Thoughts From the Chicken Bus

By Jenifer Bubenik

First published by Dog Ear Publishing
4010 W. 86th Street, Ste H
Indianapolis, IN 46268
www.dogearpublishing.net

ISBN: 978-160844-052-8

This book is printed on acid-free paper.

This book is a work of non-fiction.

Printed in the United States of America

To DKL,

for encouraging me to finally leave

To KAM,

for reading everything I ever wrote

And

To my parents,

for teaching me to be brave

ACKNOWLEDGEMENTS

With particular thanks to every traveler I met along the way. Thank you for the kind words and advice you shared with me; thank you for being my friend. Special thanks to the countries I visited for showing me what it was like to be a true backpacker. Thank you to Jorge, for your inspiration and support, and, most importantly, your friendship.

CONTENTS

Day 1: March 9, 2008

San Diego Airport

So there I was at the San Diego airport waiting for my flight to Belize. I was leaving San Diego to get away from my life which had been turned upside down over the last few months all because of decisions I made, like breaking up with Daniel and quitting my high-stress job.

Shifting my body in the rigid, plastic airport chair, my mind lingered off. I continued to replay the last five weeks back in my mind. Apparently, I had decided my life needed a little shake up. Just five weeks earlier I had asked my boyfriend of two years the dreaded question no man wants to answer "Where is this relationship going?" When I found him at a loss for words, I was heartbroken and devastated. With each day after the breakup I headed into a position I had long outgrown and begun to resent. I didn't want to be unhappy in another aspect of my life. It was just too depressing and after three years as a government relations staffer it was time to leave. Then that was it. What was once a life so on track suddenly became de-railed.

I cashed in my airline miles on a whim. Sitting there at my desk, with nine days to go before I had no job and no boyfriend, I logged online and realized my airline account said I could make it as far away as Central America. Really,

I had no clue where the hell Belize was, I had to find it on a map. After I decided to Wikipedia the country I realized Belize was located on the Caribbean Sea; there would be hammocks and a lot of rum. That was just the medication I needed, stiff umbrella drinks and white, sandy beaches.

Honestly, I just wanted to get away from my life. I didn't want to worry about running into Daniel, or if he might call me, or *more importantly* why he wasn't calling me. I was tired of crying over a guy who wasn't worth it. I went on what felt like a billion interviews only to be told "You were next in line." I was beyond exhausted of fighting political battles in the East Village that could not be won against the San Diego City Council. I was fed up with my blackberry consistently ringing at all hours with the same problems. There had to be a place in the world my SIM card did not work, and I believed Belize was it!

So now I was ready to go trek through Central America. I was going on the trip alone. I had no job, no boyfriend. I was twenty-nine. I was a TV show waiting to happen.

All my friends were *so excited* for me; they were calling me brave and adventurous. But really I just wanted to go somewhere that I could just be left alone. My blackberry was turned off and stowed away in a drawer back at my non-existent, Cracker Jack sized studio in the East Village of San Diego. If people wanted to find me they were going to have to fly down to Belize.

When Brian and Heather dropped me off it was like when my parents left me at college; I was excited, elated and full of adrenaline, but then they drove away and I got all scared and nervous. As I sat there waiting for them to call my zone I was about to cry with excitement and scaredness...was that even a word? I wasn't sure what lie ahead over the next month, but I couldn't wait to find out. There were some things you just had to do on your own.

Day 2: March 10, 2008

Orange Walk, Belize

Last night my plane leaving San Diego was two-and-a-half hours late due to a *fuel* problem. I arrived in Charlotte with one hour to spare and really tired. On the second flight I opened my *Lonely Planet* and tried to decide where in Belize I would go when my plane landed. Since I had booked this trip on a whim, my travel research consisted of what type of rum was being sold on the islands. Me, the planner, had not done any research! So during the four-and-a-half-hour flight I opted to freak out that I did not know where to go when we landed, or that I had no reservation of any kind for the next three weeks. On the plane the guy sitting next to me introduced himself as Juan and said he was headed to Orange Walk, a town in Western Belize to perform research at a sugar cane factory. He offered to take me to Orange Walk once we landed.

Right now at this moment I had never hitched a ride in my entire life. I didn't even pick up hitchhikers. So, I entertained this idea for several minutes, worrying that accepting a ride from Juan was a dangerous decision, and then finally concluded that there was really no reason not to. He was an interesting person and riding with him was better than riding on a bus for two hours in the Belizean rain. Plus, I had packed pepper spray and even though I was not too sure how actually to use it, I was a resourceful girl and would be able to survive; plus if I was going to die I might as well get it over with on the first day.

Riding towards Orange Walk I shared a Jeep with Juan and two other men I had never met, and by now I was really scared they were going to drive me off somewhere and kill me. I pretended to look out the window where I noticed that the road to Orange Walk was dirty, with trash piled high on all sides, and the countryside actually looked like a city dump back in the United States. There were little shacks all over the place that people called their homes. Actually, they looked half built, like someone began the process but never really finished. As if they were in the middle and stopped getting paid so they just never came back to work. The telephone poles were painted blue with Dean Barrow's name on them, swaying people to vote him in as Prime Minister. It was not until after the tenth telephone pole that I realized what these were for since the paint was desperately faded and receded in multiple spots. What kind of process was that? Painting your name on a telephone pole? I had been working in politics for years and believed we could save tons of money on campaign materials by spray painting US telephone polls. Even more though, I wondered if the government of Belize actually tracked people down out there in the countryside to see if they possessed a voter registration card and showed up on Election Day?

None of us spoke to each other the entire way to Orange Walk. It was an hour there. On my left side I held my pepper spray down by my thigh; unsure what I would actually do with it, but there was comfort in knowing that I had it within close proximity.

We arrived in Orange Walk and dropped Juan off at the nicest hotel in town. Not being within my price range, I asked the two men for a ride to another hotel, recommended by the *Lonely Planet*. Once there, the driver and his friend assisted me with my luggage, but it only took a minute to recognize the hotel was a boarded up shack. I was sensing a theme in this country. The two men began speaking Creole with each other, and even though there was an obvious language barrier, I recognized that they were saying "Well, she's not staying at the Hyatt now is she?"

Already feeling stupid and laughed at on my first day, upon their recommendation, I scored a $10/US per night room at the Akihoto Hotel. Ten-dollars fit my budget, the room looked comfortable enough, and who only knew what ten-dollars would get you in the USA. Thanking them for their generosity, I waved goodbye and put my pepper spray away.

For ten-dollars I got my own room and a mattress on some wooden slats. At check-in the owner handed me a clean white bath towel, a small bar of soap, and a key attached to a large block of wood. Behind her front desk was a small sewing machine where she was busy making curtains and other odds and ends for the Akihoto. I added a Belikin beer with my room charge, as it had been a long day, then relaxed in the lobby and enjoyed the cold drink while watching a young teenager play on an old, worn slot machine nearby. Listening to the cling-clang of the machine, I urged the owner to tell me about Orange Walk, but she was pre-occupied with her sewing, so I took my relaxed mood upstairs and tossed down my fifty pound backpack, where it promptly crashed on the floor. I had chosen to take a room adjacent to the street because although the noise would be greater, the window created a strong breeze to offset the humidity. I soon realized that this breeze would be filled from garbage from the street.

Within minutes of my arrival the sky turned dark, and thunder clapped down as if I should take cover underground.

Although the rain was throwing itself down in buckets, I decided it was now or never for sightseeing in Orange Walk. As I headed down the street, I noticed that Orange Walk was a mixture of Chinese immigrants and Mennonites. Looking from left to right, I was in awe and as I continued venturing up and down the sidewalks, I found the whole town was closed for Baron Bliss Day. Orange Walk was one of the weirdest towns I had ever been in. Even though the town swore they were home to sixteen-thousand people the streets were deserted. Attempting to get food, I found all the restaurants closed. Yearning for a burrito or some beans, the only option was kung-pow chicken. I was a slave to the Chinese food industry, having to take a seat at a lonely, pink plastic table and eat chicken fried rice for less than two-dollars because none of the Belize restaurants were in business. It was like Christmas Day in the States.

To be quite honest, Orange Walk was only one step above Tijuana. All they needed was a Revolution and they'd be set. My plan was to take the boat tour up New River the next day to Lamanai and then head to San Ignacio. I was getting out of there as fast as possible.

To help me I decided to utilize a program a friend back home told me about called Couchsurfing. Before I left San Diego I contacted a guy on the web in San Ignacio, Belize and asked him if I could 'couchsurf' with him; he had said to call him when I got to Belize. Well, here I was. As I picked up the phone and typed in the 1-800 number from my ATT phone card, I found out it was completely useless on the Belize telephones. I needed something called an International Calling Card. Isn't that what was written on the back of my ATT phone card? It said for International calls press two. But, no, the Belize people had some sort of phone I had never seen before. I now felt frustrated and stupid. I had a college degree and could not figure out the Belize phone system.

That is when I met Jorge.

He asked if I needed to use his cell phone. I wondered if it was a trick. My mind raced with ideas, 'I know it, I will use his cell phone, and then he will throw me against the bar and kill me. I know it. I have seen it in the movies.'

Punching in numbers, I attempted to use his cell phone, but it did not work. I thanked him and headed back up to my room. I locked the door and put a chair in front of it. I knew Jorge was coming to get me. I was going to die that night and I had only been away from home for one day. Grabbing my pepper spray, I climbed into bed.

In bed that night I felt lonely and lost. There was only a *Lonely Planet* to keep me company in a country I knew nothing about. I hated it there; I wanted to go home. It poured down rain all the time, and no one spoke English. (Even though the *Lonely Planet* said Belize was an English speaking country). I had crawled into my tight, black sleeping bag. There was no way in hell I was sleeping on the sheets after seeing how dirty the town of Orange Walk was. I felt small and alone. Why did I think traveling by myself, in a foreign country, was a good idea? Why couldn't I have just gone to an all-inclusive resort? Why did I have to be adventurous and backpack through Central America? I didn't even have a phone. I cut off my blackberry so no one could call me. The thought of that made me cry. If I did have a phone, all I would do is call my ex-boyfriend. And what the hell for? To say hi? Hi, I'm in the middle of Belize and I'm lonely, can you come visit?

Yes, I was an idiot.

Day 3: March 11, 2008

Orange Walk to San Ignacio, Belize

6:00 AM-I awoke to trash trucks in Orange Walk, just like Tuesday's in the East Village of San Diego. At 8:45 AM I met my Lamanai River tour at Jungle River Tours on Lover's Lane. Joining me on the tour was the guy from last night, Jorge. Jorge eyed all the *Gringos* and breathed in heavily. I could tell he was frustrated with us before we even left. But, seeing as how he didn't rape or murder me last night, I decided he might we worth getting know. We sat next to each other on the boat and he told me he was from Monterrey, Mexico, by way of Colombia and was traveling for a month to see all the Mayan ruins between Mexico and Honduras. That sounded like fun.

On the boat there were no cushions, simply 4 x 6 white boards that had been strung up to make an extra buck and provide as many seats as possible. On the way up the New River to Lamanai the engine stalled and I thought we were all going to be stranded in the crocodile infested water. After some maneuvering with the engine, we were off and rolling again. Immediately I spotted a crocodile so close to my side I thought I was Steve Irwin. Soon there were birds and iguanas, too. So many iguanas that the tour guide told me I should move to Belize and become an iguana guide. Well, I should start extending my possibilities... As we continued gliding up the river, there were hundreds of lily pads, and the guide pointed out that there were Northern Jacanas walking on them.

Like I was supposed to know what a Northern Jacana was.

Upon our arrival at the ancient City of Lamanai, we were treated to a picnic lunch before hiking the ruins. By far the most impressive was the last site, which I hiked all the way to the top. After the tour we returned to town where Jorge and I decided it was best to join up to travel to our next destination together. I had decided Jorge was most likely a kind face and a nice guy.

On the bus out of town I stepped up into the door, but there was no driver in sight, so I stepped back off and began to wait patiently. I watched as numerous people went by, passing me up like a busker playing music on a Saturday afternoon. As people piled onto the bus without paying, I went ahead and followed suit, only to get the next to last seat. I thought to myself, 'where I come from in San Diego, no one would dare enter a bus without paying, for fear of being kicked off or given a ticket by the Transit Service police.' But here, the motto was get on or get left behind. Once inside the bus, I noticed that the busses in Belize were nothing more than old American school busses, and I searched for over an hour to find my kindergarten nickname etched with a razorblade in one of the torn, musty seats. This form of transportation was commonly referred to as 'Chicken Busses.'

I studied their movements. This was what they did everyday in their normal life presence. They showed no signs of remorse or agitation. They rode because that was all they knew. There were children fresh from a lengthy school day, dressed in white and blue. The girls covered themselves with long navy skirts, the boys with navy slacks; everyone wore what appeared to have been once a newly starched bleached-white shirt, but now contained grey and black smudges from the day's events. There were elderly people, carrying bags from the market, full of bananas and eggs. Daily supplemental items that we in the States simply swing by the local 7-11 for on our way home, but in Central America it was necessary to travel hours for. My pack took up the entire middle aisle and people had to jump over it each time they wanted to pass. There was no way I was letting them put it in the back; I feared I would never see it again.

It was a one hour bus ride to Belize City and I had to pee so badly. After drinking eight liters of water that day, I decided it was worth the risk to use the public restroom at the bus station. It costs twenty-five cents to use the public restroom in Belize. Thinking to myself that people in America gawk at going to the public restroom inside the mall, yet here I had to pay to pee.

When the bus arrived for San Ignacio it was push and shove or one would be left standing. With both Jorge and me holding our packs tightly against our chests, we elbowed women and children out of the way and into the small confines of the retired US school bus door. I watched as an elderly Belizean woman that I had to fight out of the way fell backwards towards the ground and had a strong sense that I was headed to hell for the sin I just committed, so I briefly said a prayer. Even though I was eager to latch on to the bus, it appeared that I was not as fast as I thought, for Jorge and I were forced to take a seat near the back of the bus. Moments later the bus station disappeared, and we shared Oreos and a Coke while watching the sun kiss the clouds through the spit-filled school bus window. I thought to myself how shocking it was to believe that my friends in America would not even take the city public transit bus, yet here the only means of transportation was to ride in our old school public transit. Along the way I rode with the locals and I was the only white face during the two-hour journey to Western Belize.

Two hours later we arrived in San Ignacio, I met up with Michael from Couchsurfing. He and his girlfriend provided me with a room at the Parrots Nest hotel. It was a tropical paradise.

By now it was 11:00 PM-I was so very tired. But I was so very happy. Today I walked through a jungle of trees, met a new friend, and learned to ride Central American transportation. My adventure had truly begun. Before falling asleep I said a prayer to God, thanking him for watching over me today and keeping me safe; then I fell asleep in my hiking clothes of khakis and a sports bra.

Day 4: March 12, 2008

San Ignacio, Belize

Parrot's Nest was actually about ten minutes outside of San Ignacio by car. It was nothing but tiki cabanas on a river. I felt so blessed.

That morning I left Parrot's Nest and caught a *collectivo* cab in Bullet Tree Falls for $2/Belizean back into San Ignacio! Can you believe that? It was so cheap! I shared my morning cab with young boys about junior high age. They were all dressed in their school uniforms, with about two ounces of gel in their hair and even more cologne dumped on. But not the nice cologne, it smelled like the kind one would win at Chuck-e-Cheese's after saving up all one's tickets and then going to the counter to cash them in. They were definitely looking to impress the ladies! When the *collectivo* dropped them off at school, they strolled by the ladies as if they were George Clooney. It was so funny to watch.

Once in town, I walked through the tired, old streets of San Ignacio. There were street vendors selling breakfast, so I attempted to purchase a fruit bowl, but she would not accept my American money. Obviously she had caught on to the George Bush recession as well.

Today we were heading to Actun Tunichil Muknal, or ATM for short. ATM was discovered in 1989 and consisted of a five kilometer deep cave, filled with water. Located an hour outside of San Ignacio, we were expected to don bathing suits, hard hats and headlamps as we followed a guide into the hourglass-shaped mouth cave and maneuvered our bodies around a journey of shard and slippery rocks. On the way to ATM I sat next to one of the tour guides who told me all about his family. His brother was a Belizean Senator and he gave me the low-down on Belizean politics. Everyone here wants to know how the US election is going and I generally don't care, which is why I came to Belize. But I listened to him and tell him that Hillary and Obama are still fighting it out.

At ATM Jorge and I were paired into a group with a guide named Melvin. As we began down the jungle-filled path towards ATM, Melvin proceeded to give us more information then I could ever process. He was like Wikipedia himself. I really did try to listen, but seriously, Melvin, I did not bring my notepad. For one hour, our group followed him through the sub-tropical forest, which I soon learned was different from a regular rain forest. Melvin handed me a petite object that looked like an oversized nut and told me to bang it together. I felt like that mom in the *Parent Trap* when she was trying to fend off bears. On the way to ATM we crossed three rivers where the water came up to my chest and I decided that bringing my clunky hiking boots was a tremendous mistake. Taking a seat on a smooth rock, I changed into my Teva sandals, which were way more comfortable. This little expedition was turning out to be really fun, but way different from the vacation I had originally planned. The depth of the water was up over my hips, and I quickly learned that I had also not worn the right pants for today. My pants were one-hundred percent cotton and had been too large for me for years, meaning that they are riding low on my hips and with all the extra water weight they were now falling off me. I had also opted not to wear underwear that day, so the lower they rode on my hips and buttocks, the more I had to fold them over to keep from offering the entire group a seductive visual of my entire backside. Even still, I was consistently pulling them up so they did not keep lowering down over my bikini line. As I trekked through the river, I crawled over the rocks of the river and searched for my footing with each step. I did not come all this way to break an ankle in Belize. After the river crossing I zigzagged my way past leaf ants to catch up with the group. I had been positioned at the back of the pack, but there were numerous people talking and I could not hear Melvin, so I sneakily elbowed my way through to position myself near the front. We continued on through the forest and crawled into an opening where we left our valuables at a setup of a few logs and a blue tarp; this was known to the locals as Base Camp. For most people this would be a warning sign to turn around and go back to the bus. I was really worried about leaving my brand new hiking boots out in full daylight for four hours, but I made friends with a guy named Joshua who told me my hiking boots would be fine and no one would want to steal them. My heart beat fast; these were my new hiking boots which I bought out of my savings account, and if they were gone, I was screwed. I would be walking around Belize in flip flops for the next three weeks. But Joshua looked cool, and he was in my group so he could not steal them; thus, I bid farewell to the shoes near my Camelback and tied them to the shack holding up the blue tarp.

Our group walked down the long, dusty path to the ATM caves. Every time I brushed against one of the green leaves

my brain rattled as to what type of disease I would be bringing back to the United States. It would be years before I
could give blood again.

We were on our way to discover the lost world of the Mayans.
At the beginning of the ATM caves we were forced to swim
into limestone. Fair enough, I knew how to swim. I jumped
right in, big pants and all. I had brought a bathing suit, but
since the only place to change was out in the middle of everyone, I was swimming through the caves in my long pants and
black cotton t-shirt. It was too late to turn back now. Hitting
the water, my pants dove down to my knees, and I anxiously
reached down to work their way back up to my hips. As I
approached the entrance, it was an hourglass figure cave created out of limestone. Melvin told us to swim in to the cave,
so I did, even though it was pitch black and I had no idea
where I was going. Reaching a point on the right side, I could
feel the wall and secured my footing.

The next four hours were spent inside swimming around
while donning my headlamp and hardhat. *Oh my God!* To
that point, it was the coolest thing I had ever experienced in
my life! My body positioned in water the whole time, I continued deeper back inside the cave where Melvin showed us
ancient Mayan artifacts, including the remains of ceramic
pottery jars, which were traditionally used to hold water. The
group continued walking and as we did, my foot brushed near
a human skeleton skull remain. I jumped back at the sight,
but this was not the most shocking sight I would see that day.
Moments later, we were led to the remains of a Mayan
princess who had once been offered to the gods. She was
fully intact and was referred to as "The Crystal Maiden."
Believed to be around twenty years old, "The Crystal
Maiden" was most likely offered to the gods as a sacrifice for
rain. Now that I had come all this way to be freaked out and

see a human skeletal remain, I followed Melvin back through the water depths, passing through more calcite formations, before emerging back where we started.

After our group emerged from the cave, we broke out our provided lunch and were disappointed to see lonely tuna sandwiches; basically the tour group had taken two pieces of bread, slapped some mustard on there and emptied the can of tuna. My body was ravaged with hunger after swimming in a cave for four hours, so I wolfed down my two sandwiches and knew that the boys must be starving. Thank goodness I packed some granola bars just in case.

When I arrived back in San Ignacio, Jorge and I decided to sign up for the ruins at Caracol the next day. I had never heard of Caracol until he mentioned it, but the pictures on the wall looked great and there was no reason not to go. I was only on my third day of a month long adventure; I was not passing up any opportunities to not have fun.

Joshua agreed to join us for the trip to Caracol, and the three of us concluded that a bargain must be had with the tour agency. It would take some skill though, as an eighteen-year old college spring breaker donning her University of Florida gear walked in and plunked down her credit card, right in the middle of our negotiating. Since she and her spring break friends had no problem paying full price, the tour guide wanted to know why we could not pony it up as well. Well, unlike little Miss Florida, I was not on Spring Break…I had just quit my job and was traveling on savings, so any discount that he could give me would be appreciated. After what felt like hours of haggling, and me having to pretend that I was Jorge's Colombian wife, the ten-dollar discount was granted.

After all the hiking and haggling, I was drained. My back-pack was full of wet clothes from ATM, and I needed a shower to wash off whatever germs I may have gathered in the cave water. Tomorrow would be my third day of hiking in a row; my bones and muscles screamed for forgiveness. So, I left the boys and headed back to Parrot's Nest where my new friends had moved me to an even nicer tiki cabana; they were awesome!

Day 5: March 13, 2008

San Ignacio, Belize

This morning I once again awoke in paradise to the birds chirping at Parrot's Nest. I made oatmeal that I had back-packed down to Belize and ate it as I looked at the river and talked to Maya, another Couchsurfer from Oakland. We made plans to meet up tomorrow in Tikal. I spent some extra time in San Ignacio this morning getting to know the town, although this only took ten minutes as the whole town was basically three streets.

Taking a seat on the sidewalk outside the tour office, I waited to be joined by Jorge and Joshua. A newlywed couple from St. Louis perched next to me, and I learned they had recently gotten married out on Ambergis Caye before heading inland to enjoy the rest of their honeymoon. When our rickety old tour van was twenty minutes late, I learned that it was because the tour guide needed to wait for a police escort to take us to the Mayan ruins of Caracol. Wonderful, I was already feeling safe and secure as I piled on the broken seat.

Past the jungle and gravel road, we were led to Caracol, the largest Mayan site in Belize. The guide told us that at one time around 150,000 Mayans lived there. I found that pretty impressive since the entire population of Belize now hovered around 300,000. Once inside the ruins, we climbed all around Caracol and even into the ancient tombs! I was so impressed with all of these sites, and each one gets more spectacular to me. Afterwards we stopped by *Rio on Polls Waterfalls* and swam for an hour. The water was so refreshing. It felt so good against my dirty, grimy skin, and the waterfalls were magical as they flowed over the rocks.

As I backstroked, I thought how great it was to be there. Today was Thursday; normally, I would be at work planning a weekend out in San Diego. Yet, here I was floating through the waterfalls, feeling the sun burn down on my back and face. I spent a long time on my back looking up at the clear sky. The impact of where I was suddenly hit me; I could not believe I was in the middle of Belize, swimming in the waterfalls. I did not even know where these falls were two weeks ago, yet here I was. I dunked my head under the falls and let the water cascade over my head. It was so freeing to be here. There were no commitments for work or family or friends. I was finally beginning to see the light a little bit and even mapping out my continuing journey a little. I had decided that tomorrow I would continue towards Tikal and Flores, Guatemala before heading down to Copan in Honduras and back up to Antigua for *Semana Santa* celebrations. I had a friend in the Peace Corps there, and I would love to see a friendly face from home. Finally, I would turn back around and go towards the Belize islands and Caye Caulker. There was a whole world out there for me to see, and no reason to spend all three weeks lying on a beach. I could create my own itinerary and my own destiny. Who knew what else was out there to come?

Day 6: March 14, 2008

San Ignacio, Belize to Tikal, Guatemala

This morning I left Parrot's Nest after thanking Michael for a wonderful stay. I filled my Camelback and one liter of water for the long trip to Tikal. The wait for a cab was long at Bullet Tree Falls, so I was late to meet Jorge and then the wait at the automatic teller machine in San Ignacio was even longer, so it must be payday. Although, I really had no idea what day it was, apparently I had become a true traveler and assumed the lazy attitude.

We took a cab to the Guatemalan border. At the border the money exchangers latched onto us like parents to the children at Disneyland, and watched with extreme interest as Jorge brokered a deal with them in Spanish. I knew no Spanish, beyond my high school years and a few simple phrases. But as I searched my eyes on the Guatemalan border, it became quite evident to me that I was going to be lost in the country. I went ahead and changed all of my money into Quetzals, forgetting that I needed thirty-seven Belize dollars to pay the exit fee, so I had to borrow money from Jorge to leave Belize! I just met this guy a few days ago, and now I was asking for close to twenty-dollars. But since Jorge had also cashed in his Belize dollars, he was forced to exchange Mexican pesos with the handler to get me out of that country. Finally, I got out of there and they made us pay to get into Guatemala! I thought about the Quetzal thing for an hour and still had no clue how the exchange rate was working. I thought about how thankful I was that someone sent me an angel in the name of Jorge to explain it all to me, even though he did not seem too sure about money with birds on it either. Vigorously, I tried to explain to him that I was not a stupid American woman, but they really should put a sign up or something to remind travelers. And why the hell did I have to pay to EXIT a country anyways? I was FREELY leaving.

Continuing onward Jorge used his perfect Spanish to work and broker a deal with a mini-bus driver to take us to the fork in the road (that's how directions work here) on the way to Tikal. We hopped into the Guatemalan mini shuttle bus, which was nothing more than my grandmother's old mini-van sent down to Central America for a remodel. At the fork in the road we waited in the blazing sunshine for another mini-bus to pick us up. As we waited, we were joined by a few Guatemalan school girls, and I only wondered why they were not already at the school house. It was almost noon. Everywhere I go I see school kids in uniforms, but no one actually GOING to school.

The heat continued when finally the mini-bus appeared. It costs $5/Quetzals each or less than $1/US and I passed the guy a $100/Quetzal bill, which took all of his change. Each passenger looked at me like I was the rich, white, American. Little did they know I really only had three of those bills on me, so when they decided to rob me, they were not going to get much money.

Tikal was two hours from the intersection, so we decided to stop and have lunch in El Remate, a lovely town by Lago de Peten Itza. El Remate was a halfway point to Tikal, and the word village is better suited to describe its scenery. Selecting a restaurant, we sat down where I found the entire menu in Spanish so I picked out words I knew like *pollo* and *chorizo*, since we had those delicacies in San Diego, too. The restaurant sat directly on Lago de Peten Itza, so after our meal Jorge and I slipped into our bathing suits and walked out to take a swim. The water was so cold and refreshing, and we were joined by some fellow travelers from California, who had stayed at Parrots Nest with me. The world really was such a small place, as I continued to see travelers over and over in different areas. Lying on the cracked, wooden pier eyeing the surrounding mountains, an elderly Guatemalan man walked into the water and began washing himself in the lake. Additionally there were groups of horses bending their heads into the waters edge for an afternoon drink by the sand. The beauty of the lake could be seen for miles and there was a reflection of purple and green off in the distance. I never wanted to leave the place, but we were headed to Tikal, so I headed back up the path to change out of my suit.

3:00 PM-We flagged down an already packed mini-bus to Tikal. Walking towards the back, I attempted to throw my backpack down and almost crashed a large carrier of eggs, which was sitting on top of a crate of cabbage. The pack went on top of me instead, so I focused on looking out the window. The landscape in Guatemala was so stunning, made up of colorful aqua-blue and sea-green mountains, overlooking flowing rivers; I was looking forward to everything that I might see in the coming days.

Once at Tikal, Jorge and I decided to spend the night at the campground, which was a spacious, grassy area for tents and hammocks. For the price of $7.50/US tonight I was sleeping in a hammock outside the Tikal ruins. I was consistently amazed at how cheap everything was in Central America. We immediately dropped our bags off with one of the Tikal guards, and I watched as all my valuables were left with a stranger and locked inside a wooden shed.

We then rushed inside Tikal to spend the last two hours of daylight near Temple VI. Temple VI was located near the back of the grounds, and, upon entering, we found it was one of the most dangerous places in Guatemala. The *Lonely Planet* offered us stories of rape and worse, and I tugged Jorge's shoulder to tell him that we needed to get the hell out of there. After realizing this, we crunched the gravel grounds and ran to watch the sunset from Temple IV. From the view up top I was offered a 360-degree angle of three different temples, surrounded by clouds overhead resembling the color of a dark blue sapphire. Trees reached up above my head and birds flew by me in pairs as I took a seat on a stone to gather my thoughts. Thousands of miles away my friends were preparing for Friday happy hours, baseball games, first dates; yet ten feet away from me a Guatemalan park ranger held an automatic rifle ready to fire upon me at any moment. In the distance toucans chirped and the burnt orange sun set on the most famous Mayan ruin. I would never forget that moment for as long as I lived. Minutes passed while I sat there and watched the sun disappear behind a mountain far off in the distance. For the first time in several months I was truly happy. On that day there was no crying or retracing life moments in my head, no deadlines to meet. I simply thought about the magical place I was visiting, how blessed I was to be alive and thankful I was for my life. I suddenly realized it was almost 6:00 PM and I hadn't thought about Daniel one time that day. My heart was healing. As the sky darkened, I paused for a few more seconds to take in the view before the guards ushered us out.

Of course, as fate would have it, my day would never end without another adventure. Exiting Tikal Jorge stopped at Temple II to shoot night photos and the two of us became separated. My heart started to beat fast. I yelled his name. I yelled it louder. I yelled it like I shout for my beloved University of Texas Longhorns when they play the Oklahoma Sooners. He was nowhere within my voice. I was scared. Each guard within Tikal carried a gun and there had been stories of rape on tourists, so my worst fears entered my mind as night had already set in on the grounds. I busted out my pepper spray, which I was still not too sure how to use; I told myself that when I returned to San Diego one of my guy friends must teach me how to use it. I took off running towards the exit. Tears filled my eyes, and I switched on my PETZL head lamp to assist me in continuing down the rocky path. The only sounds were of my feet hitting the ground as I moved fast, but I had no clue where I was going. My guide book map of Tikal was so small, and I was so scared of a guard running up behind me that I did not want to stop and read anything anyway. I was afraid to keep yelling out Jorge's name because then the guards would know where I was. Suddenly, I rounded a bend where I spotted Jorge, who was dragging a very non-willing guard behind him. He yelled my name. I smiled and yelled back.

"Jenny," he screamed. "I thought I lost you."

"Jorge! I was so scared!" I replied.

He explained to me he was worried that a jaguar might attack me. What the hell was he talking about? There were jaguars there? I told him I was not afraid of those. I have fed them at the San Diego Zoo. I asked Jorge if his short term memory had caused him to forget that the guards had guns wrapped around their shoulders and sometimes people here get raped. He told me that he kept asking the guards if they had seen the American girl, and their reply was that I had already left. Seeing as how he did not believe them he shook his head and caused a fuss until one of them walked back with him to look for me. As we walked out, the two of us joined up with the rest of the sunset watching tourists and the guard in back indeed had his gun close by his side. Deciding that we should be up front, just in case he became trigger happy, the two of us ventured to lead the pack out of Tikal. I did not want to be the first to get shot. After the little adventure we decided to treat ourselves to a BIG meal at the only restaurant near Tikal and I ordered a banana milkshake. It was not a Gallo, but it would do.

Following dinner I was so exhausted. After lathering myself in forty-proof DEET, I crawled into my hammock and placed the mosquito netting back to its original position. One hundred feet away were two guards standing post outside the door of the restrooms, so I chose not to go there alone. I had to pee so badly, but even Jorge told me if I went alone then I was braver than he thought. I laughed and said one scare a night was enough for me. We swayed back and forth in our hammocks very quietly, reliving our day to each other, laughing a lot. It was nice to have a travel buddy, someone to be adventurous with. (Even if he did almost get me killed that day.) Counting out my bird money, there were only so many Quetzals left, so falling asleep in my hammock that evening I prayed for an ATM in Flores the following day.

Day 7: March 15, 2008

Tikal, Guatemala to Copan, Honduras

It was somewhere in the middle of the night that I heard howler monkeys high above my hammock. I thought they were jaguars, and since I had no reason to believe otherwise, it was not until early morning that I was corrected and unafraid.

5:15 AM-The USA hippies and Couchsurfers said "Are you awake?" Well I was now, thank you very much! Jorge and I entered into Tikal at 6:00 AM to see the Grand Plaza and were met by thick, white fog everywhere. Yesterday the guards were pushing for kickbacks to come in early, but the fog proved it would have been a waste to pay them off and come in early to watch the sunrise. Guatemala was so corrupt. Everywhere I turned people had their hands out. We had already paid our twenty-dollar entrance fee to Tikal, but the guards wanted more for a sunrise view.

Prior to leaving camp we paid a campground guard named Enrique to watch our bags and reserve us a spot on the 8:00 AM mini-bus to Flores; but when we arrived back at ten till the hour, he told us the bus was already gone. A war of Spanish words ensued between Jorge and Enrique, with me nodding along as if I understood everything that was happening. Just as Enrique was ready to give us our money back, the bus pulled back around.

Taking a seat up front, with my legs positioned on either side of the stick shift, it did not take long to decipher that the driver was the 'Romeo' of the town. Within minutes we were off to Flores, with stories of his women. The van was full of those little stuffed animals one plucks out of crane machines, all hanging from his rearview mirror and thumb tacked to the ceiling. 'Romeo' told us that each one was for a different lady whom he visits at all his stops, then he handed me his musical CD collection, each cover depicting various Latina women in bikinis and less. Along the way to Flores we picked up about twenty more people, all fitting in an early 1990's model Dodge mini-van. The sliding door opened, passengers hung on to the side and rooftop, babies piled onto one another; if you could hang on, then you could fit.

9:30 AM-We arrived in Flores and bought tickets on the 10:00 AM bus to Chiquimula, a town near the Honduras border. We paid twelve-dollars for the first-class bus, which was simply an old US Greyhound that would take eight hours to travel down the border to Chiquimula. The ticket seller told us to go ahead and get something to eat; he would save us two seats. Searching up and down the streets of Flores for food, all I stumbled across was an ice cream stand. It would have to do. I was starving. Twenty minutes later we piled onto the bus, where there was only one seat left. The lying bastard. Stepping across, I positioned myself on the hot cloth seat and threw my pack behind the driver's seat. Jorge stepped back in the aisle, where he would end up standing for the first three-and-a-half-hours.

Along the way we stopped every thirty minutes so the ticket taker could visit with his 'girlfriends' in each town. Of course, there was plenty in it for him. Through my grime ridden window view I watched as he collected bags of fruit, *Coca-Cola's*, lunch plates, and even once stopped to have a beer. Our bus was soon pulled over by the Guatemalan police who headed onboard with their massive artillery and forced all passengers off into the blaring heat while they searched the bus. Being my first bus search I began to wonder what they would do to us. I half expected them to rob us of all our money and leave us on the side of the road. I had already begun to sweat back in Flores, and by now I was doing my best to look presentable on any level. Until this point I had only seen scenes like this in movies, so I just assumed they would confiscate my US Passport, and I would be stuck in Guatemala forever. Taking refuge by a sidewalk taco shop, I looked on as the police pulled up doors and windows of the bus, asked questions of all males on board before finally allowing us all back onto the bus and the steady thump-thump of the wheels began once more.

As we continued down the road, the passenger next to me began a conversation. I had been sitting next to a Holland tourist who was headed to Rio Dulce near the town of Livingston, Guatemala, on the Caribbean side of the country. The day before we were driving through, four Belgian tourists were kidnapped and her face was ghostly white with worry. We had chosen not to stop in Rio Dulce for that particular reason, and she was quite interested in whether or not I knew anything of the political climate there. Other than the fact I had a newspaper with the event on the cover, I did not know anything, but I did know that if four Belgian tourists were kidnapped the day before, I might be geared to change my plans. Right at that moment I was thankful my friend had talked me into bringing my IPOD, so I turned it on, tuned her out, and dozed into a nap. When I woke up, I enjoyed the countryside and watched the Holland tourists head off into Rio Dulce. Jorge bounced down into the seat next to me, and I took the opportunity to teach my new travel buddy how to play Go Fish for a while until we came to a stop in a little town outside Zacapa, Guatemala. Now, all I had eaten was an ice cream bar at the first bus stop in Flores, so at this point five hours into the trip, my stomach was begging me to feed it. Outside the bus I spotted a woman on the street slicing watermelons; after flagging her down, she slid some of the luscious fruit to me through the window for less than fifty-cents. I devoured them. Pink watermelon juice ran down the front of my t-shirt, but I did not care. The watermelon was warm from sitting out in the sunshine, but I ate it anyway. Then I leaned back and wondered why I ever decided to come on this road trip to Honduras.

Exactly eight hours after we left Flores, Guatemala, we pulled into Chiquimula, Guatemala. Immediately I recognized it as the dirtiest town I had ever been to in my life. Stepping off the bus I noticed that every man in town was severely inebriated and it was only 6:00 PM on Saturday, and not a single man had a shirt covering his exposed beer belly. Walking past them they stood in packs, and my blonde hair attracted quite a crowd although it was pulled tightly back underneath a baseball cap. Jorge pushed me through the streets as fast as possible since we both realized that Chiquimula was no place for a white female, blonde, from the USA...I did not care what the *Lonely Planet* book said. Loud whistles and cat calls filled the air; those did not bother me as I heard them in the states, but there was really no reason to hang out in that town. Rounding a corner, we obtained the last two seats on a shuttle bus to Copan Ruinas, Honduras, where we stared at each other as if we had just fought a war and were the only two survivors. Jorge leaned over and whispered to me that he also witnessed a guy being chopped with a machete outside of a bar. On the shuttle bus we met three middle-aged women from the United States. I could not believe they were traveling alone and was still in utter disbelief that I just passed through that dirty-ass town.

The road to Honduras offered a prime sunset over the mountains, and I could feel the fresh air brushing against my face; how magnificent. The stench of Chiquimula was all over me, along with dried ice cream and remnants of watermelon, and I was embarrassed for other people to see me like that. Five miles before crossing into the border of Honduras, our driver turned around and told us there would be no taxis or shuttles to town, but he would continue to drive us to Copan Ruinas for fifteen-dollars per person. He was a lunatic, as we all knew that fifteen-dollars was the same price to travel the full trip from Copan Ruinas to Antigua. Fearful looks filled the three American women's eyes, and they seemed to be intimated by the driver. I did not speak his language, but I refused to be outwitted by this fool. I would spend the night at the border if I had to rather than pay the guy an astronomical fee. After some negotiating for the whole group, Jorge talked him down to seven-dollars per person. Let it be said that I still believed that the price was too stiff, but the three American women paid a great portion of our difference for the negotiating.

At the border, the Honduras Immigration official was in no hurry, and then I watched as he simply wrote my name in a notebook, accompanied with my passport number. Living in a nation where I must give my social security number for a discount card at the local grocery store, imagine my surprise when I crossed a border, and there were no hoops for me to jump through. As soon as we were back on the road, the Honduras police pulled over our bus to inform our driver he had to pay to let us continue on. Amazingly, the driver turned around and attempted to make us pay. Now let me tell you that if he wanted anymore money out of me, he was going to have to rip my bag apart to find it. As the driver turned back around, the police shouted to him "NO!! You must pay, not them," so, then I felt it was a pretty fair deal. Overall, the driver was a bad negotiator he should have incorporated that money into the first deal. By now, I had been traveling for twelve hours and smelt worse than when I finished the San Diego marathon. Just get me to that Copan Ruinas town!

8:30 PM-We arrived in Copan Ruinas, Honduras, twelve hours after we left Tikal that morning. Walking to a well known hostel by the name of Café Via Via, their dormitory was full. There were more hostels across town, so Jorge and I trekked on; I continued to lug my backpack, beginning to regret traveling with my own snorkeling gear and Travel Scrabble. What the hell was I thinking when I packed?

Down the cobblestone streets of Copan Ruinas, we arrived at a hostel named La Manzana Verde. There were only two beds left. After more negotiations we gained them both for four-dollars each, so I got the big double at the same price. What the hostel manager did not realize is that we would pay any price right then because I was not walking anywhere else, and at that point I would sleep on a rock.

I dropped my bags and dug into them for my bar of soap and shampoo. FINALLY…A SHOWER! My mother might disown me if she had seen me right then. I stunk! Standing in the shower, the water stood over my ankles while I scrubbed every piece of my body and some new ones I did not know I had. The water was like ice crystals against my skin, but after the day I had, it felt perfectly satisfying against my skin. I brushed my teeth, I used mouthwash, and I placed gel in my hair. Catching a glimpse of myself in the mirror, I almost did not know the person looking back.

There was a *fiesta* in Copan tonight at the Plaza Square, so Jorge and I headed over. We purchased some pork kabobs with tortillas, refried beans and salad from a Honduran woman's street stand, and two beers before taking a seat on the sidewalk. I had not eaten anything but ice cream and watermelon so the food and beer went down quickly, and I soon headed back for seconds. I attempted to order the second round of beers, but the Honduran men were so focused on flirting with me that gaining a beverage could take all night. My traveling buddy was forced to take over. As I polished off my second round, I was surrounded by townspeople dancing and chatting the night away. Two clowns came up and urged me to celebrate with them; I watched as they made the young children balloon animals. I was falling in love with this town. It had a wonderful colonial charm, the streets were uneven cobblestone, and there were lanterns adorning each building. All the men were dressed in cowboy hats, and there was music blaring, dancing taking place. I was reminded of a Texas street dance.

Speaking with the locals that evening, they informed us that tomorrow there would be a huge market and procession for Palm Sunday to begin Holy week, as well as the crowning of a beauty queen. It seemed we had arrived in Copan Ruinas at the perfect time.

We lingered a little longer and participated in the evening's celebrations before heading down the street to Café Via Via which doubled as a nightclub. Inside, I noticed it was very Americanized; they had *Rockstar* and *Pap's Blue Ribbon*. I laughed heartily as I looked up and spotted a silver disco ball hanging from the ceiling. Candles illuminated the dance floor, and strobe lights blazed from numerous directions. The two of us took up space near the bar on some red velvet cushioned seats for one more drink to celebrate our hard travels. I began to tell Jorge about Saturday nights in San Diego and he shared his life in Mexico. It was a pleasant evening in a fun town. People watching in Copan was magical, there was an extraordinary mixture of locals and travelers. Watching them interact in lively conversations and seductive dancing was a splendid way to pass the time.

As we walked back towards the hostel, the crowd had withered, but there were still a few Hondurans singing and dancing and consuming the last of the beers they had purchased. They knew how to have fun. I definitely liked the town and could not wait to see it in the daylight.

Day 8: March 16, 2008

Copan, Honduras

5:00 AM-I was woken up by my Mexican roomies in their attempts to catch an early bus. I pulled the blanket over my eyes until 8:00 AM when I rose and decided to eat at the market. The colors of fruit and vegetables were radiant although I was first greeted at the door by a man with a machete chopping off any type of meat I could ever imagine. Taking a seat on a small plastic, blue stool, I ordered scrambled eggs and black beans with a side of tortillas. I accompanied my meal with a Pepsi. Pepsi was everywhere there and Jeff Gordon could be an ambassador to Central America. All of this costs me less than $2/US. Across the table from me sat the mother of the cook. Throughout breakfast I made conversation with her, and she shared with me that she and her family lived an hour-and-a-half away. Her profession was the town midwife, and in the last five years she had delivered sixty-five babies. This was not her full time job though, as she also worked in the coffee fields for less than two-dollars per day. Astonishment took over, and I found myself doing the math for every four-dollar mocha I threw down for at a corner coffee shop. It would be impossible for me ever to walk into a coffee store again without remembering her face. During her story she explained that everyone in her town worked in the coffee field and the coffee owner provided various necessities for them. Void to the Spanish language, the conversation was taking place entirely with Jorge translating between the two of us, while he developed less patience with me and my need to learn Spanish.

I told him it was not that I was not willing; he is just a bad teacher. We had been traveling for seven days and he had not taught me anything.

The procession did not arrive until well after 11:30 AM, at which point we had taken up refuge in the back of the water truck directly across from the Catholic Church near the main plaza. We were tired and cranky from spending two hours out in the Honduran sun. We began to see hundreds of persons walking towards us in the street; all the people from the surrounding villages flooded into Copan holding palms, many tied into the shape of a cross. As they descended into the church, we followed and positioned ourselves in back to listen to the beginning of mass. Mass was entirely in Spanish, but the emotions of the ceremony were on such an amazing spiritual level that it was easy to chant right along. From wall to wall, the church filled to capacity, so we did not stay long, allowing others to take over our spots.

Afterwards we walked north out of town to the Mayan site of Copan, where the ancient city once stood. The remains left were unbelievable; the carvings of the ruins were so intricate and detailed. I was astounded by the stone sculptures that lay before me. Site Stelae C was my favorite with a turtle shaped altar. On the way out of the ruins we spotted a family of Guacamayas, and I snuck up close as they ate their pineapple. Amazing creatures I watched as they snacked and flew off in pairs through the willowing trees of Copan. Leaving the ruins we also met up with the three American women who were on our shuttle into town. I listened as they told me about their tour guide for the ruins. The one woman said "He was a real bullshitter." It sounded like money well spent to me.

Walking back to town there was a gathering on the right side of the road so Jorge and I headed over. The area was covered by yellow beer tents reading *Imperial* on them. After assessing the situation, it turned out to be a cockfight ring. We decided to stay and watch. This is the type of event I would never be able to see in America, and I knew some of my friends would not agree with my attending. With the number of vegetarians and vegans in California, they would have PETA down in Copan tomorrow. The audience was made up of the top men in Central America. Immediately, I noticed that I was the only woman, and the attention eyeing me could be dangerous. I offered Jorge a story; we would tell them that we were journalists sent to Honduras on a story. It was unlikely that they were going to ask for badges or business cards of any sort. We sold our story good, so they allowed us to get up close and personal and take lots of very good photos…even holding some of the roosters. As a journalist, all of the men in Honduras believed I was important and did not mess with me; I was like a queen. When the ringleader placed the rooster in my arms the arena erupted in whistles and claps. I immediately wondered what kind of diseases I picked up while there. Looking over I saw Jorge bent over laughing at the attention I was bringing to the show, but at no time did I feel unsafe. Walking into the back of the event, I eyed roosters being sewn up after fights they had won, to allow them to continue fighting. I watched as boys as young as ten placed spurs on roosters, to insist that the rooster claw his way in the next fight. Blood filled water buckets, and then dead roosters were taken out back and made into soup for dinner.

Speaking with the men who ran the event, we found that every weekend the cockfighting changed towns. There was so much money running through that place, while right outside people were forced to work for nothing. Hearing the money exchanger discuss the process depressed me and only reiterated how far Honduras had to come to bridge the monetary gap. I heard him tell us how the day before five-hundred-thousand-dollars had been wagered by men, mostly area drug dealers. He then smiled while flashing a giant stack of bills out front.

Continuing our "journalistic" research, we had some beers while talking with the men in the crowd. They informed us that the next day would bring a rodeo and then the crowning of Miss Copan. Thanking them for the information, we began to head back to town. On the way I noticed the large number of uniformed Honduran police officers, and I told them we were journalists and would it be okay if they considered a group photo with me? They agreed and I snapped a picture of me and the five Honduran *policia* before my confidence wore off. During our walk back into Copan, Jorge and I decided that we would stay two more nights before heading to Antigua. I could not resist sightseeing in this town! I had fallen in love with Copan! It was so cute, and the architecture was amazing.

After the cockfighting ended, I headed to the bank to take out some more Lempira's and the receipt read invalid transaction. Apparently I had taken all of the money out of this country. The money in Central America is so out of whack, but it is so cheap here I could live forever!

Deciding we would have to live off the Lempira's we had, Jorge and I headed across town to a bar called the Red Dragon. Walking up the stairs, I was met by the sounds of Motley Crue and Snoop Dog. It was so Americanized that the bartender was dressed in a Coronado Shores t-shirt. Noticing his blonde hair, I looked him in the eye and asked him if he was from California, to which he replied "Do you know where Chico is?" For a moment I considered smacking him upside the head, then decided against going to a Honduran jail, even though I was now on friendly terms with the police. Rum and cokes were only one-dollar at the Red Dragon, so after two long hard days I drank plenty of them while sitting on a tall bar stool overlooking Copan Ruinas. Simply minding my own business and sipping my drink, the town Gringo transplant began to hit on me. I hated to be the bearer of bad news, but I had not come all that way to get hit on by a retired veterinarian from Colorado, although my travel buddy thought it was hilarious. Jorge was of no assistance at all, and I was left stranded up against a wall while the guy shared with me how he left Colorado to live in Copan and install cell phone towers. Really having no interest in him, I continued to order rum and cokes, while changing the subject and inviting Jorge back into the conversation. The local guy provided us with some "insider" information, since he noticed us two "journalists" at the cockfight earlier today. The retired veterinarian he is, it is his job to sew up the roosters for the townspeople here. He seems to take great pride in this work.

After another few rounds, he sends us to another local bar, confirming that there will be much more of an authentic feel. My eyes were a little blurry at this point, but I had my pepper spray and Jorge to protect me; ten minutes later both of us realized we were walking across a skeletal bridge, and the darkened sky contained a dangerous feel. I shared with Jorge that I was going to die because this is where the locals send blonde, female Americans although my words came out more like a shout since I was pretty drunk at that point. Deciding the walk was not particularly safe, we turned to head back to the Red Dragon where the local *Gringo* guy had moved on to a teenage Honduran girl. Meeting new friends, we closed down the bar, so late in fact the Chico bartender handed us our last beer in a to-go cup and kicked us out as he closed the door on my ass, even though it was only midnight. On the way home I walked straight past the hostel and the night guard laughed as I stumbled in.

Day 9: March 17, 2008

Copan, Honduras

This morning I had a slight hangover, but it was nothing that the cold hostel shower water couldn't cure. This morning was so hot, we went to the Hotel Maya to use their pool-there was a sign welcoming us and asking us to please leave our guns at the front desk. Awesome. It was only too bad that I did not bring my gun that morning.

Entry into the pool was two-dollars. With the sunshine blaring down and sweat covering my body, I would pay two hundred-dollars right then. There were two guys there whom I suspected were drug dealers as they were the richest Hondurans in town, but they had three cute kids, so I played with them until I fell asleep under the trees. I was getting as dark as my Colombian buddy even though I consistently lathered on the SPF thirty.

The kids came back over and pulled me into the pool. The youngest boy was fascinated by my toenail polish. A cherry red color, I smiled at him as he counted each of my toes over and over. Days ago I had decided that the pedicure was a waste of money since I had been wearing my hiking boots everyday, but seeing him take such an interest in my feet changed my mind. I started to play airplane and Marco Polo with the kids, and we clapped and splashed around until it was time to leave. I thoroughly enjoyed my time at the pool. It was just the refreshment I needed from the Honduran sun.

Back at La Manzana Verde, it was time to dress for the afternoon rodeo. Attempting to look as unattractive as possible, I put on my khakis, an old, faded Banana Republic t-shirt and my San Diego Padres baseball cap. No make-up. Two blocks away in the Main Plaza, there was a truck blaring with super-sized speakers tossed up on top. Two men inside told us we could hitch a ride down to the rodeo park with them. Good because it was hot. Once at the rodeo, we grabbed some lunch of carne, salsa, tortillas and the excellent Honduran beer of *Imperial.* I made a note to find it in the states upon my return.

At that point I was the only woman in attendance, and believe me I was working very hard to look my worst everyday. There were more police at the rodeo than in the San Diego Gaslamp on a weekend, and their guns were amazing. Many people in attendance were at the cockfight yesterday and recognized Jorge and I as the "journalists." Keeping an eye on the bulls, I watched as they got revved up and strolled over to the ring where I began to take my journalistic photos. Watching the cowboys as they changed their clothes, I recognized their muscles to be phenomenal, and I spent extra time perusing close to their circle. As the crowd continued to filter in, we were joined by last year's rodeo queen, and finally a little tuk tuk, complete with bull horns on the front. Just like in Texas. Announcements began, and singing started; it was none other then the winner of the Latin America American Idol.

Unfortunately, the voice coming through the microphone was one of the most unfavorable I had ever listened to. Throughout all my years of patronizing karaoke bars, this singer topped the list of bad singers. After he finished and the cowboys draw their placement numbers out of a hat, more music started. Alan Jackson and then the 'Gambler' by Kenny Rogers blared through the scratchy old speakers. I loved it. I knew every word and could dance the Texas Two Step, but I really hoped it was not how the Honduran people learned their English, by listening to Alan Jackson sing 'Chasing that

Neon Rainbow.' After watching five bulls I decided to head back to town. It was hot, and tomorrow would be a long day traveling to Antigua.

Day 10: March 18, 2008

Copan, Honduras to Antigua, Guatemala

4:30 AM-The rooster crowed and I wanted to kill it. I went ahead and got up, then left some words of advice in the hostel guest book about steering clear of the local *Gringo* men. In the shuttle mini-bus the driver packed twenty-seven people inside, not counting the three babies that were kicking and screaming or the two guys hanging on the top railing; their machetes weaved back and forth in the loop of their jeans.

Back in Chiquimula we connected to another bus that would take us to Guatemala City; it was only 7:00 AM and I would have given anything for a shot of espresso that morning. A *Coca-Cola* had to do, and I settled into the seat behind the driver for the three-hour bus ride between Chiquimula and Guatemala City. On the way we passed vehicles like a NASCAR driver, and I was certain the end of my life was near. Once arriving in Guatemala City, smog filled the air. It was dirty and polluted; traffic consumed the streets, even though an industry friend back in San Diego swore to me that Starwood Hotels possessed a Westin property there somewhere. Recognizing a sign for McDonald's, I was obviously back in civilization. This was a prime opportunity to patronize the golden arches, so at the bus stop, we headed right into McDonald's and I immediately ordered a Big Mac. After one and a half weeks of traveling, sometimes one just needs a taste of home. Standing at the counter I emptied my pockets to pay the bill, and the manager reached over to grab my hands. Rattling off Spanish words I didn't comprehend, he suggested that I get control of my money. Looking down, I only possessed one-hundred Quetzals, or thirteen-dollars, but by his standards one would have thought I deserved a spot on *Lifestyles of the Rich and Famous.* By the time I took my red plastic tray to the table, my eyes were swarming with tears at the thought that I couldn't even eat fast food safely. To my right stood an armed security guard ready to pistol-whip any-one who robbed the franchise. Once back outside, a scumbag taxi driver refused to give us directions to zone three, which was where the bus to Antigua was, and my eyes were glued to how disgusting Guatemala City was. Standing in the middle of zone one, taxi drivers withheld information needed to all tourists, simply to receive a few Quetzals as reward for their good doings. Their eyes addressed what their mouths did not as I felt them undress me with every turn and step I took. Several minutes passed before a taxi agreed to drive us to the bus station and hopping in the back seat my fingers immedi-ately pushed down the broken, cut off locks. No one else was getting into that cabby. I zipped my mouth shut as the driver began shouting about how much he hated Americans. He believed Jorge and I to be married, which would suffice as long as I lived to see another day. Gazing out the back seat taxi windows, I witnessed firsthand drug dealing, armed criminals and poverty living on the streets of Guatemala City. The only thing I wanted was to be out of that town, right then.

Arriving at the bus stop, my backpack barely fit in the rack above my head, but I was not letting it out of my sight. Thoughts raced in my head that I must be in a red zone from the Department of State and somehow missed the warning. Continuing into Antigua, the old school bus was already cramped when one local forced herself into our two-person seat, settling into our laps. The three of us sat on the tiny, worn bus seat for over an hour while numerous sales people entered and exited the bus with such frequency that often I did not have time to observe what they were selling me. A mother pushed bubblegum on passengers so that she may feed her children and a twenty-something male dressed as a clown skipped up and down the aisles showing his magic tricks to all that would watch. Chickens and ducks squawked from the rear while biblical preachers stammered out the word of God.

In Antigua, we lugged our packs across the busy afternoon activities, scouring the streets for a hostel. Knocking on door after door, eventually we stumbled upon a place to stay, despite being told the city was sold out four months ahead for *Semana Santa*. Tired and agitated from the day of traveling, we threw down our bags without even securing the name of our new lodging. Hoping to catch the afternoon light, I headed to Parque Central in the middle of Antigua, and started snapping photos. I could not resist using an entire memory card; Antigua was breathtakingly stunning. Lamp posts, water fountains, architecture, cobblestone streets; it could have been Charleston. From my viewpoint in the center plaza, I saw countless churches. I began snapping photos of them when a little boy ran by me with a stolen camera. Starring in disbelief I double looped my camera around my hand and slid it into my pocket. The young boy joined his friends, and they laughed jovially and took turns playing with his newfound prize.

Because it was still early in the day, we visited Iglesia de San Francisco, Catedral de Santiago, and Iglesia y Convento Nuestro Senora de la Merced. I also spotted the Palacio de los Capitanes. Known as the Palace of the Captain General, the building has been repeatedly rebuilt following numerous earthquakes and was once the seat to the Spanish Colonial Government. Since I wanted to hike a volcano, we checked out tours in various offices, but were being hounded by a vendor on the street. Offering us a seven-dollar deal the next day, he was the sketchiest guy anywhere. Not too convincing, he walked us into another tour company who vouched for him. His name was Manuel and after some bargaining, we went ahead and booked with him, paying forty-Quetzals to hike Volcano Pacaya in the morning. Manuel wanted the name of our hostel; looking at each other we shrugged our shoulders and questioned one another as to who knew it. Truthfully, we did not even know what street it was on since we just left our bags and hit the town for sightseeing. Using the small map of Antigua, we attempted to point to an intersection. Manuel nodded his head in agreement and told us he knew precisely where the intersection was, and he would see us at 7:00 AM tomorrow morning.

That evening I just wanted to get clean; I was so filthy and dirt remained all over my body. I wanted to put on some real woman clothes and feel like a lady. I needed a manicure and pedicure. Apparently ten days without makeup was my limit because all the other girls in Antigua looked like as though they fell out of bed without trying, and I looked like the smelly backpacker I was. So, I headed back to the hostel and took a nice shower, cleaned up and put on the one dress I was backpacking through Central America with. Trying hard, I applied the little makeup I brought and blow-dried my hair with my travel dryer. This did little to help me, and I still had to accompany the dress with black flip flops, but I felt a little more attractive. Heading out to dinner, Jorge did not recognize his backpacking buddy. Chuckling, he told me he had only a few hours before he must get Cinderella back to the hostel. Doubled over in laugher, I told him, yes, at midnight I became a backpacker again. For dinner we headed to *La*

Fonda de la Calle Real, where I attempted to order a martini. We were in the middle of Guatemala, but the menu said they had vodka, so I believed they could make it happen. The waiter returned offering his apologies that the bartender had no clue what a martini was. I asked if they had olives. He left. He came back; they had olives but still do not know what to do. I tell him I would take a margarita. Jorge explained to me the waiter was so embarrassed he did not know how to make my martini; I told him I would have made it myself if they let me.

At dinner Jorge told me he was going to teach me how they eat in France-without rushing. I said ok-that is why I came on vacation, to stop rushing my life. He say's he's already noticed that I've stopped doing that since he met me, so maybe this trip is making a difference.

After dinner I come back to the hostel and go to the roof, look up at the stars and the volcanoes. I was very thankful to be there, for all the new friends I had made and the great time I was having.

Day 11: March 19, 2008

Antigua, Guatemala

Once again my TIMEX was set for 5:30 AM, but there was a rooster crowing long before that hour. Rolling over I looked at my watch, and it glowed brightly 1:30 AM...I was going to KILL that damn bird and make him into soup. He crowed all night. Finally, my alarm went off, and it was time to hike the volcano. Excitement filled my body as I dressed in my dark green cotton shorts and new hiking boots to experience some-thing I had never done before. That morning we would be attempting *Volcan Pacaya*. Located halfway between

Antigua and Guatemala City, *Volcan Pacaya* is an active complex volcano, meaning it has more than one feature. The volcano last erupted violently in 1965, with streams of continuous eruptions since then. Frequent armed robberies have plagued the volcano, advising tourists not to head up alone. This is why we had chosen to patronize Manuel's services as opposed to tackling the hike on our own.

6:30 AM-We were still waiting on the corner for the shuttle bus. I was sure that guy Manuel took my money and ran off. The streets were cold and deserted. Last night's litter fluttered in the early morning wind, and occasionally we saw other vans drive by, but they continued on without stopping. It seemed we had been left, and Jorge and I began to discuss ways to kill Manuel. Finally, our van pulled up, already packed with tourists. Looking at them, I recognized that everyone had packages of food but us. We had not consumed breakfast, not even coffee that morning. Manuel did not say anything about needing food today. Peeking at everyone else's Styrofoam boxes filled with beans, tortillas, and fresh fruit, something told me I was not prepared for the volcano hike at all. Why had I not thought about bringing food? Filing in to the van, the drive was long; Manuel did not say anything about a long drive. He just showed us pictures of smoldering orange lava and giant black rock. Even though *Volcan Pacaya* is centrally located between Antigua and Guatemala City, we were basically heading all the way back to Guatemala City. We were also passing a lot of restaurants. My stomach growled loudly, and I could tell it was upset with me for not feeding it that morning. This day had quickly changed from eager anticipation to anger and resentment.

Finally, I spotted a turn-off road, and the group arrived at a shack. I asked where the restrooms were located, and a little girl said, "Follow the chickens." Laughing uncontrollably, I completed her instructions, and it turned out not only were there chickens, dogs sized me up, too. Since my German hostel roommate believed she had contracted rabies after being bit by a dog the day before, I attempted to keep a clear distance from the furry animals and avoid being pecked by the chickens as well. This was hilarious. As I peed, the chickens continued to look for an opening through the two swinging doors and I was in and out of there in record time.

The hike to *Volcan Pacaya* began, and I listened as the guide spoke only Spanish. Dazed and confused, I wondered where the walkie-talkies were. Cursing Manuel for not making me aware of the situation, I began the assent through a light green forest and manure-filled dirt road. One of my group attendees had chosen to ride a horse up the path, and every few minutes the four-legged animal stopped to leave a pile of stinky steamed manure along the way. The woman on top of the *caballero* was of a higher-class and did not seem to mind that the horse's droppings were ending up all over me. I notified her to stop, and I quickly passed on the right. The hike was slightly strenuous which Manuel also did not mention as he was swindling me on the street. This was all topped off by the fact that my Camelback was not completely full of water. Halfway up the trail we approached a clearing and observed the volcano from a distance. Cotton-ball shaped clouds moved throughout the light blue sky, allowing us to observe the summit more clearly and take in all its beauty.

Moving forward on the trail, we entered into a wide open field, full of wildflowers and livestock. It led us towards the summit of the volcano, and the smoked-filled air was very harsh on my lungs. Touring *Volcan Pacaya* was definitely dangerous as I was soon climbing over heated lava, which was very sharp and jagged. No waivers were signed before beginning this tour. If we were in the United States, I had no doubt proof of health insurance would have needed to have been shown, along with a ten page form proving no lawsuits would be filed upon our injuries. When I reached the flowing lava, my legs felt as if they were going to peel off. The tour guide poked his walking stick into the red, burning fire, kicking the flames up even more. People's shoes began to melt. My face was blistering, burning with heat, and I removed myself by twenty-feet from the center of the flames. Watching the rest of the group, others continued closer to the lava, and the guide explained that the lava was over two-thousand degrees. As they rejoined me, I was dumbfounded at how amazing the experience just was. I could barely believe I had just hiked a volcano in Guatemala!

After returning to Antigua, a group from the volcano decided to go out to lunch. Throughout the ride back to Antigua I had read the *Lonely Planet* for an hour to research where we should take lunch and studied the map of the city. Walking the streets through Parque Central and into the Eastern section of town, we found no restaurants, only boarded up homes. Locals poked their heads out of windows and doors to share with us that the restaurant we were looking for closed three years prior. Once again, the *Lonely Planet* had sent us on a wild goose chase. Agreeing that there were a large number of restaurants back near Parque Central, we carried our backpacks the opposite direction and settled upon a quaint lunch spot where we enjoyed beers and tacos. Tired and hungry, the items went down quickly, and I leaned back in my chair to catch my breath for the first time that day. There were only a few minutes to rest; however, because the children of Antigua began partaking in their *Semana Santa* procession. Boys were dressed in deep purple robes and girls as young as newborn infants could be seen in white lace dresses. Old men donned black suits and carried band instruments as the music began to fill the streets. Small adolescents carried a makeshift coffin so big they nearly toppled over, and I followed the procession for several blocks, mixing in with the devout Catholics and random tourists. The crowd was so grandiose that it was necessary for me to carry my backpack on the front of my body so as not to be robbed. For in every direction I watched young men eyeing the crowd and made sure to pocket my camera in a safe spot. Hours later the procession continued through the streets of Antigua, wrapping around each block until every corner of the city had been covered. As the event dwindled, purple hooded participants faded into homes, and old men carried their instruments behind their shoulders. Confetti covered the streets, and a heavy trace of incense filled the night air.

At 6:00 PM, I returned to the main plaza and searched for my friend Pamela. Pamela was currently living near Antigua working with the United States Peace Corps. We had not seen each other since August of the previous year, so once we spotted each other, the hugs were long and hard. She introduced me to her friend Kevin, and the three of us headed to a bar called Kafka, where we picked up Jorge on the way. Kevin told us he knew of a Cuban band playing salsa nearby, so we headed over and danced until 1:00 AM. The beat and rhythm was loud and fun, and the dance floor was packed; the *cuba libres* and *Brahva's* were flowing, and all individuals on the dance floor that night were full of congenial spirits. I was in dire need of some salsa lessons, and Jorge pulled me onto the dance floor. My Colombia buddy shook his hips from left to right and placed his hands on my waist in an attempt to follow. Anyone who had ever danced with me knew I was not a good follower, but with the salsa beat so easy to enjoy, I found myself swaying late into the night. The music is amazing, the dancing is hot and sensual and I was having a great time. As patrons dwindled we moved closer to each other. If I had just met this guy I would be dancing more seductively, but he was my travel buddy. Then without notice he pulled me into a corner and began kissing me and I decided *what the hell- we're only together for two more days.* He was 24 and I was 29; the make-out session lasted a long time before we closed out the dance floor and headed home. As I climbed into bed and fell asleep I thought 'What a great day.'

Day 12: March 20, 2008

Antigua, Guatemala to Caye Caulker, Belize

Roosters crowed every fucking morning in Guatemala. They would never make it near my house as I would ring their lit- tle necks before they ever had a chance to wake up for a crow. Exiting the *Los Amigos* hostel, where I finally learned the name of my sleeping place, I met Pamela for breakfast Pamela and she showed me her favorite breakfast spot in Antigua, named *Dona Luisa's*, where I had pancakes and rel- ished every bite, appreciating that I was not confined to fruit or a Guatemalan burrito. Pamela gets a cheeseburger, since it's very seldom she can eat those. Drizzling butter and syrup throughout the stacks, she and I caught up with each other, while discussing Guatemalan and Central American politics. For two strong, independent American women, it was hard for us to watch the female gender so repressed throughout Guatemala. Pamela and I discussed this topic a while longer until our faces were so flushed and hot it was imperative for us to change the topic.

Soon after we walked throughout the streets and witnessed artists painting sawdust and flowers for an afternoon celebra- tion. Artists had worked for up to sixteen hours to sketch and design the patterns, and their hands were stained from the long hours of work. Individual carpet colors consisted of royal purple, deep red, sunshine yellow, and lush greens. Patterns depicted such designs as crosses, flowers, and hearts. Hundreds of tourists had lent a hand on the projects; the street crowds were comparable to the Fourth of July on popular beaches in the States. Perusing the streets I was amazed at how much radiance and splendor filled Antigua. It was truly spectacular to visit the city during this time of the year.

6:00 PM-Jorge and I had arranged for a bus to Guatemala City, but at 6:30 PM we were still waiting. When the driver finally pulled up he instructed us to follow him twenty blocks to the other side of Antigua, and I had now officially walked ALL OVER the city. My body was fatigued and depleted from thirteen days of traveling, trekking countless Mayan ruins, bargaining over hostel rooms and I was just ready to return to Belize and arrive in Caye Caulker, where the hammocks and rum were waiting. Isn't that why I came on this trip in the first place? Sitting behind me in the shuttle was an amusing woman who shared her experiences of the last few weeks; they mimicked mine, and soon I was laughing right alongside her. Being reminded that with every bad encounter comes a story to laugh off or share around the Thanksgiving table simply made the long ride better.

Once in Guatemala City, we were dropped off at the bus station to connect in Flores. Again, I took notice that the city was dirty and dangerous. The streets were gray and frigid; *tiendas* were shut down with thick bars covering their front doors and windows. Guatemala City offered nothing but a connection to tourists, who could only hope for a safe one at that. Sitting in the front seat of the reformed Greyhound, I stared out the window and realized we were behind schedule. In Spanish the driver told all passengers there was a 'problem' with the clutch. Jorge relayed this message to me, and I once-again vowed to become fluent in Spanish back in San Diego. The driver began to edge the broken bus forward and proceeded to journey around the block twice before heading back to the station for maintenance repairs. Oh, Lord! What if something happened to me? Of all the places I could die, Guatemala City sure as hell was not at the top of my list. Two blocks later we were sitting back at the bus stop when a mechanic headed on board with a large tool to fix the clutch. I would gladly walk back to Belize right now if I could. Sensing my fear, Jorge began to make jokes when a Guatemalan man dotted in tattoos jumped onto the front of the bus. Sharing a story about how he was recently deported from Orange County, California, back into Guatemala, he questioned whether we could help him out with some money to return to the United States. Looking me square in the eye, this question flew out of his mouth. If it was not the clutch, then certainly I was going to be shot by this ex-gang member. Twisting my head from side to side, I assertively told him 'no,' and he stepped off the bus. Praying the driver closed the door, I leaned my head against the cold window and soon we left the city. Scared for the first time in over a week, I experienced one of the worst nights sleep ever. I had slept in a lot of different places...airports, tent camping, aunts' and grandmas' floors...the road between Guatemala City and Flores was windy, bumpy, frigid, uncomfortable, and I just wanted the hell out of Guatemala. I was fed-up with men totting guns and machetes; worried about being robbed everywhere I turned, mathematically trying to solve the Quetzal figure in my head. How long was it until I got to Caye Caulker?

Saying *adios* to Jorge at the Guatemalan border, he ventured on north to Mexico while my path went east to the Cayes. My eyes were fuzzy at 4:00 AM as we hugged goodbye, and I thanked God as I watched him drive away in a separate van. Only thirteen days before I had been alone, wondering where to go in Central America, lost in a country with no friends. Scared of his 'hello' at first, we were now good friends, a history of laughter and stories between us. Promising to visit each other in San Diego and Monterrey, my knees buckled back onto my backpack, and I tried to find some shut eye while waiting to head towards the ocean.

Day 13: March 21, 2008

It took me nineteen hours to get from Antigua to Caye Caulker between yesterday and today. Two buses and one water taxi later, I rolled up to the beautiful Caribbean seaside island, and five steps off the boat I walked into *Tina's Backpacker Hostel* and grabbed my tiny, but cozy, bed. Nothing more then a slim mattress and one purple sheet, it will have to do for the next five days as proximity to water won out.

Amy, who checked me in said her husband is taking a boat out at 2:00 PM so I could go. I grabbed my snorkel gear and went in search for food. I found a BBQ selling chicken, rice, and beans and brought it on board. All the other passengers are jealous, but I hadn't eaten since Antigua almost nineteen hours ago.

That afternoon I snorkeled two popular coral reefs and followed it by swimming with sting rays. One of the scariest things I had ever done in my life, my heart was beating as my captain advised me to dive off the boat backwards and stand in the sand flipper-less. As he threw sardine chunks into the ocean, I watched in amazement while I was joined by forty or so stingrays. The animals paraded near my ankles before the captain captured one of the animals under the stingray's lateral fins and brought him slightly above the water for all of us to pet. Feeling their skin was like touching a smooth velvet jacket. Scared in the beginning, the captain calmed all my fears, and being so near the stingrays was a joy of my life. Chasing them around like a small tot chases Santa at Christmas; I could not wait to tell others about my once-in-a-life-time experience.

At the end of the evening I pulled out my North Face sleeping bag where I tucked myself in. I listened as the palm trees swayed outside and the waves crashed into each other. Thankful I was no longer in Guatemala, Caye Caulker was the tropical vacation I hoped for thirteen days ago when I flew away from San Diego.

There could only be better days to come here in paradise.

Day 14: March 22, 2008

Today I woke up and did nothing.

Lured to the Cayes by sunshine, pina coladas, and hammocks, I won the lottery today by sleeping late, then lounging around in my bikini. There were no roosters outside my window or gun totting Guatemalans. Promptly throwing on some sunscreen and taking my towel twenty steps out to the pier with my new read, I found a home for a few hours. Caye Caulker did not possess white sandy beaches, so locals and tourists alike found themselves stretched out on wooden piers half completed that extended into the crystal blue waters edge. Walking to the end of the island brought one to an area the local's called "The Split." The Split divides the island in two, offering a dredged out waterway and sandy bank for persons in need to lie down on. More for children looking to test out their latest blow up toys, I chose to steer clear and located myself right near *Tina's* pier. As the day progressed and my body temperature got hotter, I moved to the shade of the hammock and listened to my I-POD while dozing in and out of sleep. The beach in Caye Caulker was lined with hammocks, and I took the time to people watch as individuals hopped in and out of the tree swings all afternoon. Time was of no importance out on the Cayes which gave way to my simply saying 'later in the day.' I watched boys catch live Barracuda and baby nurse sharks with their bare hands ten feet away from where I rested. It was like *Survivor*. Skinning them in front of my eyes, they joined several other guys from the hostel to light up the rustic, timed-out BBQ while several other girls and I made rice and potatoes. Within hours we enjoyed a feast as the sun went down. Over the course of the day I had become friends with another traveler named Kristy. Together, we set off to the Bamboo Bar, where the floor was beach sand and the chairs influenced by wooden swings. Taking up space in them we rocked back and forth while ordering pina coladas and listening to the beats of reggae music pour through the speakers. Bamboo Bar was not packed, but the vibe was exactly what I was looking for. The walls were constructed with tiki poles, and the pina coladas were two for the price of one. Looking around the Bamboo Bar, it seemed like the kind of place that could be hard to escape, and I knew now why so many people had told me they had been on the island for more than one week.

There were many sights I wanted to see while on the island, but I only had a few days left. Tomorrow I had arranged for another full day of snorkeling to Turneffe Atoll where we would have the opportunity to view sea turtles. I had been reading about the Turneffe Atoll for a week and a half now since traveling. Stretching thirty miles long and ten miles wide, Turneffe is a twelve-acre island. Consisting of creeks and lagoons, the area was home to millions of crabs, shrimp, turtles, and other aquatic species turning the Atoll into a Disneyland for divers and snorkelers alike. The boat would leave at 9:00 AM, and I surely did not want to miss the experience.

Heading home, I set out my equipment and bathing suit so I would be ready first thing in the morning.

Day 15: March 23, 2008

Early morning-I had stopped keeping time so I wasn't really sure of the hour, but I knew it was time for a full day of snorkeling. After quickly dressing in my bikini and tossing my snorkeling backpack over my shoulder, I strolled down the street sans flip flops only to be informed that my tour had been canceled. The tourist office was a small, blue building, and the owner, a large, round Creole woman. With a Caribbean accent, she tells me, "Don't worry, man' you can go tomorrow." But there would be no tomorrow for me since my time on the island could not be extended. My three week airline miles ticket was coming to a close.

Looking around, I saw another young woman from the hostel heading towards me. She informed me that her tour had been canceled, too. Together we strolled over to Tsunami tours and signed up for a 9:30 AM snorkel trip that would carry us out to Swallow Caye for manatees, Shark Ray alley, and Caye Chapel Aquarium. While waiting, she shared with me she had been traveling the world for two years, including stopping here and there to give back with volunteer work. Burnt out on her job back in London, her travels were coming to a close but the experience had been fantastic. My head began to spin with ideas of returning to San Diego, packing up my apartment, and traveling the world.

On the boat ride to Swallow Caye, the guide passed off the stern and let me steer the boat. Nervous at first, I thought how it was a good thing a friend back in San Diego let me steer his sailboat from time to time, so I was prepped me for this little side show. People actually thought I knew what I was doing and were impressed with my transportation skills.

Meanwhile, I was terrified I would wreck us into an island. Our first stop brought us to Swallow Caye, an area covered in mangroves, south of Caye Caulker. After sitting in the boat very quietly, we spotted five manatees and one dolphin so big I mistook it as a shark. He frolicked and played with us while we observed him swimming in and out of the mangroves. The tour lead on to St. George's Caye for lunch, a secluded island that is the type of place one heads when one is really looking to get away from it all. St. George's Caye had no grocery stores, and the locals whispered that the homes do not go for less than one million. Picture postcard, surrounded by palm trees and stunningly clear Caribbean water, St. George's Caye is an island retreat unlike any other I had ever set my feet upon. It was nothing less than beautiful.

Settling by the pier, I enjoyed a fish sandwich and a FANTA, truly the "official" drink of the islands. This small island had not been destroyed by tourism and the outside world, and I lounged around finding the stunning views worth every penny the residents paid. The most spectacular point was that even the less fortunate, like me, could relish in nature's beauty, by simply jetting over on a small boat. Leaving the magnificent island, we headed to the outdoor attraction of Caye Chapel Aquarium for more snorkeling. Coral in that area included radiant colors of purple and gold, and I was astonished at how grandiose each piece was. I swam slowly, taking my time to relish in all the beauty under the sea and headed down so deep that my ears started to pop, but I wanted to see the fish! Fish in all shapes and sizes surrounded me and disappeared deep into caves and crevices; I followed until all that was left were tails disappearing into dark holes. Blue chromis were my favorite creatures; however, we also spotted a sea cucumber, and finally sea turtles which I was allowed to hold. Our tour traveled to Stingray Alley again; yet this time I was not afraid of them anymore and was surprisingly calm as I jumped right in and found my way over to the school! On the way home there was a cool, tropical breeze, and the afternoon ambiance was very peaceful. There were not a lot of boats populating the waters that afternoon and I could see for miles into the open ocean.

Later in the evening I gave out travel advice to people heading towards San Ignacio and Tikal. Fifteen days ago I didn't know anything about this country and now I was giving out information about it! Hostels to lodge at, chicken busses to take…I was awfully proud of myself. Definitely not the lost girl with the *Lonely Planet* that I was when I landed; afraid to accept a ride from a stranger. Something in me had changed. For someone who had never even used their passport before, now I felt like a seasoned traveler. Was that a funny statement to say?

Day 16: Monday, March 24, 2008

Rain was pouring down outside. I rolled over and look at my watch; it read 5:00 AM so I drifted back off to sleep.

At 8:00 AM I woke up and found a strong breeze outside. For my final day on the Cayes, I decided to go exploring the island. Caye Caulker houses were not really houses; just more Belizean shacks-wooden 2x4's placed on top of four poles. Painted bright colors of turquoise blue and flamingo pink, it was a crayon box gone wild. Everyone had their laundry hanging in their backyard, and trash littered the street. This was the part not written in the travel books. There was trash everywhere. If the second largest barrier reef was not just a mile away, this island would certainly never see tourism. Stumbling upon a blue cottage with the name 'Glenda's' painted out front, I peeked inside and stayed for a while to enjoy some warm, homemade coffee and a cinnamon roll for seventy-five cents. Glenda's was busy, as locals hopped in and out for breakfast, not staying longer than to pick up a plastic to-go bag full of warm, piping cinnamon rolls.

Since it was a rainy day, I finally had the opportunity to use the travel Scrabble I had been lugging around for three weeks and a few of us played a round before we went to get some ice cream. After the rain subsided I searched the island for some food and come across a little place named *Syd's*. They are famous for their fried chicken dinner which I attempted to order but the guy tells me it will take almost an hour. So I splurged $18/Belize on the shrimp platter, which still took forty-five minutes. It comes with mashed potatoes almost as good as my own and for a moment I thought Syd had stolen my recipe. There was a creepy guy next to me who kept trying to make conversation, at which point I must write that every man on this island is either a local or an American transplant-retired, divorced, or forced to move here because of the restraining order put on him by his ex-wife. After he got the point I was really into my shrimp and not him, I finished enjoying my meal and headed back to bed where I fell asleep reading.

Day 17: Tuesday, March 25, 2008

I signed up with EZ-BOYZ tours to sail towards Hol Chan Marine Reserve, Shark Ray Alley, and the Northern Cayes. On the trip out, the water was choppy from the wind, and I got scared as we bounced up and down. Closing my eyes, I imagined my tour guide Salvador was really George Clooney from *The Perfect Storm* so that when we sank it was George I was going to die with, not Salvador. We ended up making it to the Northern Cayes safely although I was beginning to ponder swimming back on my own. There were seven people on my tour, one guy and six women they were all from Canada and I, the lone American. After hopping in the water, I realized that my day was about to be spent in a huge grown up aquarium! Saving the best snorkeling day for last, right away I spotted fish so big they did not fit in the lens of my camera! Salvador led me to more green moray eels than I could spot, and I realized this was a great spot to search out my favorite underwater creature, the blue chromis. There was something called a peacock flounder, which floated on the bottom and was just as beautiful as the bird. Just as I was enjoying all of this, the Canadian guy kicked me in the face with his flippers. Okay, once no harm, but then he did it four times! So did the other family members; if you do not know how to snorkel, then do not come. You did not see me heading to Canada and riding a moose, did you? Pissed off and angry, it was doubtful he and I would be exchanging emails after the day was over.

Our next stop was Shark Ray Alley; we had been told there were nurse sharks and as soon as we pulled up, they swarmed the boat. The Canadian wife screamed, "I'm not going in there!" Good, more for me to photograph! Jumping right in, I soon realized what the hell I just did. There were seven nurse sharks right beside me. Okay. Just breathe. Turning around from my spot beneath the ocean, I quietly and swiftly moved towards the rudders and treaded lightly as I waited for the Captain to jump in. He was busy trying to coax Little Miss Canada into the sea, and I was about ready to toss her in when she finally changed her attitude and gradually slid down the back ladder. Following the Captain at a more gingerly pace, I witnessed him catch a nurse shark with his bare hands and swam over to the group for a petting exercise. No thank you. I watched Shark Week. I knew what happened. Continuing on, more stingrays followed, and twenty minutes later when I got back into the boat, I looked behind me just to make sure "JAWS" was not back there.

Just up the ocean, we found our last stop at Hol Chan Marine Reserve, the first marine reserve established in Central America. The park encompassed about five square miles of protected area and was one-hundred feet deep in some parts. It was dotted with coral formations, and I felt like NEMO. Spotting the biggest fish in my life, like grouper and barracuda, the main thing I noticed was the hundreds of schools of fish. Schools of fish were so abundant and magnificent; often times I mistook them for coral formations. Far down below, there was a cave Salvador instructs us to swim through, but I could not hold my breath that long. In fact no one could but Salvador. I had learned to pressurize my ears, though, so I was able to swim deeper and get better photos. As I swam out far away from the boat, I suddenly came to a one-hundred foot drop off, which sent fear running through my spine so I thought it was best to turn around; who *knew* what might be lingering out there, looking for my yellow fins?

When I returned to the island, I found that a BBQ was planned at the hostel for everyone's last night, so I showered and cleaned before we all headed out for a market excursion in search of fresh vegetables. Within one hour there were twenty of us, from various nations, peeling potatoes, chopping onions, mixing rice. Someone plugged in his I-Phone into some speakers and the dancing started. A party was going on; stories were flying, and friendships were being made. Tomorrow, I would leave Belize; most of my new Caye Caulker friends would head to Western Belize or North to Mexico. That night was the perfect way to end my time on the island.

Part II

I arrived home to San Diego at the beginning of April, 2008. I swore my studio apartment was cleaner than when I left; perhaps it was that I had been looking at chicken coops and farms for a month. Whatever it was, it was nice to be back, and I gladly took a nice long shower in my own place, with my own towels and large bottles of shampoo. No more travel bottles. No more worrying about having the water shut off at 10:00 PM.

Lying in my studio apartment that first night, I immediately decided to return to traveling. There was a bug that got sparked in me along the way, seeing new sights, meeting new people, learning new things. After talking to so many people from around the globe, I wanted to be part of something bigger. Figuring I would never have the opportunity again where I was not tied to a job, a husband, or children, I knew it was now or never. My savings had a reasonable amount left that would allow me a few more months of fun, depending on what region of the world I chose to visit.

This time traveling would be different. I would bring something back from the trip. I would learn a new language, conduct volunteer work. Listening to other traveler's experiences that they had shared with me, I wanted to give back to society and be part of something bigger. I already volunteered in my own community of San Diego; why not offer my skills somewhere else?

Upon looking closer at my budget, I set a timeline of one month before leaving San Diego. I had to give my notice at my apartment and close out odds and ends. I planned to travel until year's-end; therefore, I would be traveling for six more months when I set back out. There were a lot of things to take care of. For starters, I needed to decide where to go. Australia had always been at the top of my list, but the plane ticket alone would consume most of my budget. Europe would be cool, but with the rate of the dollar at the moment, there was no way I could live past a week. China entered my mind because of the close proximity to the Olympics, and it was still pretty reasonable monetary wise to visit. Finally, I decided that I would fly back down to Central America and finish what I started, and really learn Spanish while I was at it. I sent a few emails out to friends letting them know of my plan and quite a few emailed back stating they knew people in certain areas and could help with my planning. That was a great place to get me started.

I also had to start packing up my place. After living in the same studio for close to four years, it was a mess of grime and dust balls. But now, it was all those things, plus banana boxes and dirt. I had already made two trips to the Salvation Army and had begun selling my life on EBay. I could not really figure out the Shipping and Handling though, so who knew if I was really making money or not. The important part was that I was ridding my life of filth and dirt.

A lot of people kept asking me how I was able to afford taking the rest of the year off and going to travel. Over the last three years, I had worked extremely hard to put away enough savings for a rainy day. While all of my friends were busy driving their cars around and forking over ridiculously high gas prices, I walked to work every day and took public transportation. They all laughed at me when I said, "I have to leave early because the bus is coming." But who was laughing now, when all that money I saved got put into savings and I was able to take a year off and travel and they were still stuck at work. I thought of that one morning while I was at the gym, in the middle of the day, enjoying the treadmill while there were no crowds around. Each day at least three of my friends asked me how I was able not to work and I thought how easy it is when one modifies his lifestyle down to simplicity. I would not be traveling extravagantly; my budget was going to set me near $28/US per day. I would be staying in hostels and Couchsurfing wherever I could.

One day while I was packing my phone rang. It was the nurse from the Kaiser Permanente travel advisory department. I needed some more vaccines before I went off trotting through South America. She asked me to please list all the countries I planned on visiting one at a time. I rattled off about nine and ended with Australia; she said to me, "that's the only safe country." I laughed to make conversation, but thought to myself it was really none of her business where the hell I went, so could she please just order the yellow fever vaccine? She asked if I was traveling for business or pleasure, and I told her for pleasure. That I was just going backpacking, but I might do volunteer work in Ecuador if the opportunity arose. She asked if I was a missionary. Um, no, far from it, but why can't ordinary people do good work? Why did you always have to be sent on a mission?

Part III

Day 1: May 25, 2008

Managua, Nicaragua to San Juan del Sur, Nicaragua

I was in Nicaragua. Never in my life did I ever think I would
visit this country. I landed here after flying on TACA out of
LAX through El Salvador. Flying out of LAX had saved me
one-hundred-dollars, but never again would I fly out of that
airport. It was a nightmare from the moment I got dropped
off at the curb. I was the only single, blonde, American
female in line and thanks to the three-ounce rule the United
States Department of Homeland Security had installed I *had*
to wait in line even though I only possessed three bottles of
DEET. I was forced to wait behind numerous persons checking so many bags it made my head spin, and I was ecstatic
that I had gotten to the airport earlier than the required three
hour time slot.

Landing in Managua, I recognized that the Managua airport
was the most efficient I would encounter on my travels to
date that far. There were state-of-the-art computers, and the
border officials were dressed similar to military guards in the
States. My face filled with excitement as I was ushered right
through the front of the line. The border official politely
asked, *"A Donde Va?"* Since I had been practicing my Spanish in San Diego, I was finally prepared for this question and
properly responded to her with "San Juan Del Sur." I was so
excited to be able to respond back with the native language!

Pulling a five-dollar bill out of my wallet, I paid the country entry fee and watched as she stamped my passport. I was free to enter Nicaragua. Exiting the customs area, I could not see through the row of Latin faces in the airport. Hundreds of people awaited their families' arrival from the United States. Pressed against the glass windows, people of all ages, genders, and sizes held signs, balloons and flowers for their loved ones. As fast as the security doors opened, they ran and held each other in bear hugs and slobbery kisses.

Passing by the crowd, I glanced around for my previously arranged shuttle. It was nowhere to be found. This allowed for one too many taxi drivers to attempt to pawn their services off on me, and I spent my first hour in Nicaragua fending them off like flies. By the time the shuttle arrived, I had taken refuge in a corner of the airport, make-shifting my backpack into a stool of sorts. Climbing into the shuttle I was thankful to find it contained crisp, cool, air conditioning as the humidity in Managua was stifling.

The decision to visit Nicaragua was supported after meeting a young woman in Guatemala who relayed a story about a volcano she hiked on Isla de Ometepe. Her description sounded majestic and adventurous and extremely dangerous. She was from France and while sipping coffee together in Antigua, I explained to her that French and American passports looked very different when traveling through Latin America. Working in politics, I had participated on a case involving an American living in Nicaragua. During 2006, American Eric Volz had been sentenced to thirty years in a Nicaraguan prison following his conviction for the rape and murder of ex-girlfriend Doris Ivania Jiménez in the tiny beachside town of San Juan Del Sur. Researching his case, I knew that Nicaragua was a dangerous country and could be very unwelcoming towards American citizens. Taking all of this into account, I had studied maps of Central America and knew that returning to the area meant a possible visit to the country. When it came time to make the decision of where to study Spanish, I was reminded of my conversation back in Guatemala and relished to see the beauty of which she had spoken so fondly of.

With over a year of research completed on the Eric Volz case, my plan had been to stay away from San Juan Del Sur and wonder through the *calles* of Grenada instead. This would allow me to take full advantage of the colonial atmosphere and cafes that so many travelers revel in. Sharing the idea with a friend, he coughed up the fact that we currently had a mutual friend living in San Juan Del Sur. I agreed to meet with him, and he convinced me that San Juan Del Sur with its laid back attitude and beach atmosphere was where I wanted to be. Over several beers he reassured me that San Juan Del Sur was safe and upon leaving my *Espanol* would be *muy bueno.* Putting my trust in him, four weeks before my arrival into Nicaragua, I had contacted the *Latin American Spanish School* to begin the starting point for my Spanish immersion. The feelings of dependency and confusion I had while traveling in Guatemala and Honduras were to be gone soon. I was here to study Spanish and participate in the Nicaraguan daily life for two weeks.

When I arrived at the Latin American Spanish School, I was greeted by one of my professors, Ana, who hugged me tightly and welcomed me to Nicaragua. Ana instructed me to follow her, and we walked through San Juan Del Sur to my host family with whom I would be living for two weeks.

I found it rather exciting to be back in Central America, beginning a six month journey, mastering a language I had

waited so long to uncover. Strolling through San Juan Del
Sur, I took notice of the dirt streets, numerous Internet café's,
and abundant surfing shops. Past the Texaco stood a run-
down bicycle stand where a group of Latin men stood holding various tools and paint cans. Directly past them on the
left, Ana led me into a house that had two hammocks and four
rocking chairs out front. Four women waited for me and
delivered giant smiles as I walked up. Producing some of my
new Spanish, I replied, *"Es un placer conocerles y su
familia"* and *"Hablame de su familia por favor."* Loosely
translated this meant *it is a pleasure to meet you and your
family* and *please tell me about your family.* Laughing, the
host mother gave me a hug and responded that my Spanish
was *muy bueno.* Fatigued by the long travels, I settled into my
room for a nap. The room consisted of four sterile white, tile
walls, one poorly stained from a roof-top rain leak, a simple
full mattress and two thin pillows, a pink plastic chair and a
box fan. The bathroom was outside, an outhouse of sorts
with cold water to keep one clean. After settling in, I was
handed a pink slop-bucket to do my business in at night. That
would be my home for the next two weeks.

After my arrival it rained all afternoon, and I used the time to
unpack. When it was time for dinner, I still did not know my
host family's last name, but all of the women were named
Maria. The family also had three sons, all of whom were now
living in the United States. Inside their home was covered
with photographs of the boys and their American wives and
children. Throughout my time in San Juan I would come to
find out that the parents had never been to the United States
to visit their sons, but loved listening to stories of life in
America. At dinner the first night, there was an obvious language barrier and while I dined with the two youngest girls,
our conversation consisted of what I could point out from my

See it and Say it in Spanish book. Luckily, I did know when they asked if I wanted *cafe con leche* for breakfast tomorrow morning. To which I replied *"Si, muchas gracias!"*

Tomorrow I start classes at 8:00 AM so I turned in early.

Day 2: May 26, 2008

San Juan del Sur, Nicaragua

5:00 AM-The roosters were back, and there was a parrot living outside my door. Added into the mix was a German Sheppard waiting for me every time I went to the bathroom. Watching him watch me, I was eternally grateful I went through with all those rabies vaccines. The only English the parrot knew was "Hello Jenifer" after he heard my guest mom say it. It cracked me up!

By early morning I had started my Spanish classes. As the only student there, I received one on one lessons from my *Professora* Victoria. Victoria was a patient and kind teacher. She was a beautiful Latina woman, with long, thick, jet-black hair and a heavy accent. To begin our lessons, she asked me questions such as *Do you live alone, Are you married, Do you have a husband/boyfriend/kids?* I explained to Victoria that yes, I lived alone, and there was no marriage/husband/ boyfriend/kids anywhere in my life. She wanted to know why. She wanted to know how old I was. Why was a woman at the age of twenty-nine, living in America, as beautiful as me not married? Although I did not say it, I wanted to tell Victoria, "I do not know, Victoria. Because men are stupid, Victoria. Because I don't like children and don't have the patience for them, Victoria." The day became very intimidating very fast. Even in Spanish I had to justify my life.

Victoria taught me to say *Yo vivo sola; No, no soy casada; No, no tengo novio; No, no tengo hijos.* Meaning I live alone; no, I am not married; no, I don't have a boyfriend; no, I don't have kids; it sounded depressing, even in Spanish. Living my entire single adulthood as an independent self-sufficient woman, listening to my Nicaraguan Spanish teacher ask *Por Que, Jenny, Por Que* was quite depressing. Having no real reasons to answer her other then *Just Because* we were suddenly stuck having to change topics. I directed Victoria to teach me everything I ever wanted to say about my family. By the end of day one, I was flawless at sharing anything about my brother Chris and my sister Ashley. Victoria said my Spanish was *muy bueno*, which I was led to believe meant all of her other students must either be totally worthless or I was better than I believed. Handing me a healthy dose of *tarea*, Victoria scooted me out the door. Striving to be the perfect student, I practiced my Spanish homework all day as I lay on the beach. In early afternoon the sun finally came out, but not until after I learned the word *lluvia*, or rain. The thick drops caused a high tide to come in and the surfers flocked to the waters. San Juan Del Sur was a surfer's paradise, and every other person in town was a Gringo surfer from the USA. My trip through town earlier had helped me to discover the town itself was nothing more than a few streets, but it possessed a beach, so it worked for me. The sand was a little darker and dirtier then I had hoped for, mimicking a muddy grey stone color, while possessing sand flies. I realized I was being bitten on my ankles and retreated home to practice my verbs with ten-year-old Maria, who had no problem correcting me when I faltered. We played charades together, and I enjoyed the game to help me learn. Still, it was humbling being schooled by a fifth grader. Following the night lesson, I tried to teach her to play 'Go Fish,' but would have to wait until Victoria taught me the Spanish words for Ace and King so we could have all the rules firmly in place. Watching Maria attempt to count the cards and numbers, I began to notice her lack of educational skills. It was clear that she knew numbers and colors verbally and could count to ten on her fingers, even higher to twenty in the marketplace. Yet, as we played with the cards, her hesitation to recognize a number placed before me was imperative. Perhaps it was not my Spanish barrier causing the problems between us, but her utter failure to understand what was in front of her. Wishing her goodnight, I headed to my room and turned on my I-Pod. Attempting to stay in a somewhat positive physical condition, I kneeled down on the hard floor for homemade yoga and push ups. It was nearly impossible to keep the weight from adding to my body with numerous portions of rice and beans entering my mouth each day. After a few repetitions, I decided to call it a night, knowing the roosters would come calling soon enough.

Day 3: May 27, 2008

San Juan del Sur, Nicaragua

There were ants in Nicaragua and they loved *Gringo* skin. I was being eaten alive, and concluded to go on the counter-attack with my forty-proof DEET. Turning everywhere I would see ants marching on the ground, up walls, and across window sills. Two new words had also entered my Spanish vocabulary; *cazar* and *gallo,* because I was going to hunt the roosters that woke me up all night long. Every morning right outside my window the roosters crowed at 5:00 AM and rose me long before the sun broke into the day. I was compelled to string them up.

Continuing my studies, Victoria quizzed me on my Spanish reflexive verbs, and not too surprisingly the ones I picked up the fastest were *bailar, cantar* and *llamar.* Then she taught me numbers up to one million and quizzed me. I tried to explain to her I did not even know how to write over one million in English, much less Spanish, but she gave me a bunch of *tarea* anyway and pushed me out the door. Included in the price of my school fees were additional activities such as cooking and dance classes. I began my first activity learning to cook *arroz con leche.* Within minutes I concluded we were making basic rice pudding. Still new into the Spanish language, I began the class by trying to write down all the words the teacher spoke. Her accent was heavier than a bag of ten pound oranges, so I reminded myself that back in America we have regular access to the Internet, and I could just Google the recipe. Cooking on an old green camping stove, I watched as she mixed milk, rice, sugar, and cinnamon together and then stirred rapidly so as not to burn the finished product. Sampling the dish was a fun way to end the day, and the sweet dessert melted like warm chocolate between my lips.

Day 4: May 28, 2008

San Juan del Sur, Nicaragua

So apparently I have a career in meringue dancing if becoming a bilingual politician does not work out. Victoria said my hips don't lie Shakira, although my tango needs a few more lessons. I told her I was waiting until Buenos Aires to get some up close and personal lessons on that one. Also, last night I spent hours studying Spanish numbers during a homemade gym session. I would count in Spanish while performing jumping jacks, sit-ups, push-ups, and crunches. When I finished, I would begin counting backwards, which was much harder than it sounds. Beginning at one hundred in Spanish,

I counted back down, while jumping up and down. I would fall asleep telling myself that that counting would help me when I was bargaining at the *mercado.* All of the counting did pay off as I did well today on my Spanish numbers quiz. Victoria said I'm doing well, except I can't pronounce *viente* correctly, so I hope that I never have to order anything that costs twenty-dollars. I blissfully blame it on one too many Starbuck's encounters

As I sat down to finish my nightly study Victoria came knocking on our door to tell me class tomorrow would be canceled because her *hijo y hija* have *escuela actividas.* She asked me to please come, so I will visit the school for parties and take the day to look around town and study.

Day 5: May 29, 2008

Hurricane Alma decided to visit Nicaragua at the same time I was there. This morning I woke up to *mas lluvia* and simply thought it was a bad storm. Before falling asleep the previous evening, Victoria had paid a visit to let me know class would be canceled in honor of a Mother's Day presentation at her son's school. She had invited me to join her at the San Juan Del Sur primary school the morning of May 29, so I proceeded to get dressed in the one semi-formal, black and white dress I stowed away in my backpack, brushed on makeup, attempted to look presentable, and trekked my way through town. Except that San Juan Del Sur was **FLOODED,** and I was the only one on the streets. I carefully journeyed across San Juan Del Sur wearing my knee-high dress, black thong flip-flops, hot pink rain coat, and my Camelback. As I turned up the first street past the Texaco, I was met by a gully wash of water as high up as my knees. Ready to turn home, I kept going because I promised

Victoria that I would come to the program. Water was flowing in every nook and cranny of San Juan Del Sur; the rain drops pelted against my jacket and into my eyes. Blinded by the storm, I aimed for the right side of the street where a few houses owned awning. The sidewalks were slick as molasses, and I removed my flip-flops to avoid a fall. When the sidewalk ran out, I was back in the street, walking without shoes, my feet touching broken rocks, twigs, and beer bottles. I was in the middle of the street, walking in a river of mud and soot, working off a map Victoria had drawn for me in my journal. When I showed up at the school, I was met by twenty Spanish speaking teachers who explained to me in Spanish that the program was canceled. Pulling out my *See it and Say it in Spanish* handbook to guide me through our conversation, I found it drenched and ruined and unable to comprehend anything they were relaying to me. Free for the day, I decided to drag myself to school and study. Since the two schools were only a few blocks apart, I figured I would be able to make this trip rapidly, but I was bombarded by rain on the way, and forced to stop at an elderly lady's house. At this point of the week, my Spanish was about a three on a scale of one to ten, mostly adjectives, nouns, and numbers that one needs in everyday life. I was also excellent at discussing any family issues. The house I had stopped at was owned by a woman who had lived in Nicaragua all her life. She was elated to have me roll up on her porch for shelter and watched with interest as I cleaned off my feet and shook the massive amounts of water and leaves from my hair. Striking up a conversation, she began stirring the pot of interest and talking to me as though we had been friends for years; problem was I could only interpret half of what she said. I turned the conversation to our families and where we were from; this helped us carry on for over an hour, all in Spanish. When I left, she knew all about my brother Chris and sister Ashley.

It was only after I made it to the *Latin American Spanish School* that I discovered a hurricane was positioned off the coast of Costa Rica and Nicaragua. Oh´, so that is why all the wind and rain! It was all making sense. Good thing I wore my finest dress that day. After finally making it home, my host mom Maria asked with great concern if I was scared, and I explained to her that I was from North Carolina, and I would protect everyone should the hurricane actually be rough. Then I began to wonder how houses were built in Nicaragua and should I actually be worried about the construction of such facilities? Joining the family in the living room, we watched the news out of Managua, learning that forty mile-per-hour winds were hurdling towards the coast of Nicaragua and rising waves were off the beach. The thing that most frightened me was whether or not the house would be able to withstand any type of wind. Forty-mile per hour winds were not great in America, but the Managua news made it sound quite frightening. Two hours later, after the rain subsided some, I headed to the beach and watched the waves. They resulted in twenty foot high white-water curves, crashing down hard, and the water was rough. No swimmers dared venture into the water. Numerous surfers littered the folding foam, dotting in and out, spilling over the tops of waves.

Four hours later, I would receive an email from the United States Department of Homeland Security warning me that a hurricane was approaching the western coast of Nicaragua and that all U.S. Citizens should take precautions. I would like to thank the U.S. State Department for sending me that warning email regarding Hurricane Alma four hours **AFTER** the hurricane hit the coast of Nicaragua. It really made me feel safe to know that I still had to put all my sunscreen in a three-ounce bottle when traveling, yet I did not even know there was a hurricane hitting the country I was currently visiting.

Hurricane Alma also left the beaches of San Juan Del Sur in chaos. Walking around the following morning, I observed the damage Alma did; thankfully, no major damage had come to the town, but the beach sand had been replaced with massive amounts of broken trees and boats shipwrecked on shore. It was impossible to lye on the shore and enjoy the view for the rest of my visit.

Day 6: May 30, 3008

San Juan del Sur, Nicaragua to Finca Magdalena, Nicaragua

Today I was prepared to leave for my trip to Ometeppe. Victoria provided me with excellent tips for my trip to the fairytale island and ordered me "Jenifer, only Spanish! No English!" So, this little weekend trip would be a great test for my Spanish.

Today was Mother's Day in Nicaragua and as I walked back home for lunch the streets were flooded with guys selling stereos, TV's and a store selling red balloons and roses while blaring *Who let the dogs out?* During lunch we had *sopa* and I thought the *carne* was a cow's heart, until I finally bit into it and discovered it was a hard boiled egg yolk. Thank God! My family wished me *Buenas Suerte* and I was off to Ometeppe.

The Lonely Planet, which I had now nicknamed *The Lonely Liar,* wrote that busses left from the San Juan Del Sur *mercado* off to Rivas every thirty minutes, but I ended up waiting an hour and fifteen minutes, so once again the *Lonely Planet* was wrong. I grabbed a seat at the front of the ancient United States school bus, and once we retreated out of town, I noticed I was the only non-Nicaraguan on the bus. I figured that was a great time to practice all the Spanish I had been learning, so I struck up a conversation with the people to both sides of me. To my right was a man in his mid-thirties who explained to me that each day he awoke at 5:00 AM to catch the bus from Rivas to San Juan Del Sur for his teaching position at one of the many language schools in town. One day he hoped to visit America, but realized the great expense the country brought on. The excitement built as he found out my English was perfect, and, he begged me to teach him a few words. Telling him I had been instructed to speak only Spanish that weekend, he laughed and from then on our exchange consisted of our family issues. However, since my *viente* still possessed a Southern accent to it, he believed Chris to be ninety-seven and Ashley to be ninety-two. Finally, I was the youngest child!

Since my first trip along the road between San Juan and Rivas one week prior, Hurricane Alma had washed out what small, rocky, road had been in place. This left the bus dragging along to the right side of the muddy mess, leaving its tracks in the ditch. As we dragged through the tiny neighborhoods leaving San Juan Del Sur, the bus took up space following a bulldozer, who paved a smoother path to follow. Yet, soon enough we were playing chicken with a second yellow machine as we crossed a narrow bridge above a chocolate brown river. Closing my eyes I said a silent prayer, while feeling the bus sway over to the right, and I was almost certain we were driving on two wheels. Reaching a fork in the Pan-American Highway, I exited the bus at the Shell gas station following directions from the *Lonely Liar.* Looking around, I spotted several abandoned houses and a basic Central American bus stop, nothing more then one concrete bench covered by a cracked roof. While I waited in the middle of nowhere Nicaragua for a bus to take me two kilometers, I watched as the locals eyed me with amazement and confusion. Scared as hell standing alone on an unfamiliar corner, in the States I would have walked the two kilometers distance, but since I had no clue where I was going and was the only *Gringo* around, I was not about to set off on foot. Again, the *Lonely Liar* read that busses came every thirty minutes, but after waiting over an hour, I knew they were full of it. I had been standing on the side of the road under that blue concrete roof with Nicaraguan country people looking at me while I carried my backpack. Spotting a TV repair shop, I killed time by practicing my Spanish with the childish look- ing boy running the place. Knowing he could not be more than sixteen, his polite demeanor put me at ease as my heart continued to reach up out of my chest. Finally, I jumped into a *collectivo*, joining two men and held my pepper spray close by. Thoughts raced through my mind about which direction they could drive me to and the types of weapons they would use to kill me. After a few seconds though, the driver under- stood my directions perfectly, and I made it to the ferry in San Jorge. I had now made it from San Juan Del Sur to San Jorge for little more than one-dollar. Approaching the ferry ticket window, I began to speak to the ticket counter agent regard- ing the ferry and accidently slipped in an English word. Responding, he said 'Oh, you speak English?' Surprised at his reaction, I felt a great sense of impression. Did I look like I only spoke Spanish? All the studying over the last week had come to light, and I believed I might make it through the weekend. Attempting to ease my comfort level, he began speaking badly broken English to me. I replied, "No! Only Spanish!"

As I walked to the ferry, I observed with great fright only men aboard the big, boxy, water mobile and knew that I was just setting myself up for possible trouble. Passing by them I observed whispers and hisses, but I had to take this ferry to the island in the middle of nowhere. It was the situation my mom had warned me about. Greeting me onboard was a man who looked eager to get the ferry rolling. Paying no more attention to me than most people do to a stray dog, he pushed an ancient, cracked clipboard into my hands and instructed me to sign. After scribbling my name and country of origin on the crumpled paper, I headed below deck where there turned out to be more women setting off for Ometepe. Taking a seat in the middle of the boat, I positioned myself on the long white bench that would no doubt feel like riding on a teeter-totter for the next hour. Beside me sat six people from England, fresh off another boat from Grenada. Since we would have missed the last bus in Moyogalpa for the day, we decided upon our arrival it was best to grab a taxi together to the other side of the island.

Using the hour to train my tongue in Spanish, I chitchatted with an elderly Nicaraguan man standing near me on the boat. Soon into the conversation I found out he was from Los Angeles. Hey! I was from San Diego! After enjoying the ferry trip by telling him all about California and San Diego, I found out Los Angeles was actually a small town on *Isla de Ometepe*. Nice, at that point he must have thought I was an idiot. At any rate, we rattled on about our families, our work, and the island. Everyone in Nicaragua was going to know about my brother and sister by the time I left the country. My meticulous practice and attempts to learn family words in Spanish had definitely paid off.

Before long, the ferry was in view of *Volcan Concepcion* and *Volcan Maderas*. Gazing towards them I was met by a thick cloud of white smoke covering their cone-shaped tops. The island was covered in a dense-row of tidy trees so neatly formed that I was unable to view any homes or activity on the island. Pointing to an area adjacent to the beach, my ferry buddy flapped his arms and offered me a toothy smile. My thoughts were he was possibly offering me and my new friends a ride and knew a taxi guy. Not comprehending a word coming out of his mouth, I smiled and said, *"Si."* He looked at me as if he wanted more so I tried again with *"Bueno?"* Hoping for the best, I vowed that our group would come with him after anchoring. As we pulled up to the island, I found it stunning; brightly colored flowers lined the walkways; emerald-green trees lunged down to the ground.

After landing, there was a taxi guy waiting for us as my ferry friend had said, and the driver proposed a deal to drive our group to Finca Magdalena. I used my new bargaining skills to broker a better one, and we were off. Once in the truck I sat up front with the driver, and my new friends sat in the bed with the bags. The driver and I provided company to each other for a while before picking up his younger brother. Fourteen and nineteen, the two of them taught me more Spanish over an hour and a half then I had learned all week. Yearning to learn English, they shared stories with me of their dreams to come to America and study at a university. They attempted to learn the language from old textbooks left by professors and travelers visiting the island.

Between Moyogalpa and Finca Magdalena, the road was nothing more than a rocky mud pit of holes and vast boulders. It took an hour to travel there in the four wheel drive, stick shift, vehicle, and with every bump came a rough exchange of gears. The English group was having a tempestuous time banging around in the back and questioning how much further until the end. On the Eastern side of Ometepe, we passed though Playa Santo Domingo as the sun was setting and were greeted by a pastel pink radiant sunset. It was as though the sight came out of a movie.

Twenty minutes past Playa Santo Domingo, we arrived at Finca Magdalena. An old farmhouse set on an organic coffee plantation and a hillside, Finca Magdalena is positioned on the far eastern side of Ometepe. For $2/US I could sleep there that night. Even more impressive was that I could order my room all by myself in Spanish and that people asked for my help in translating! Before leaving, the driver and his brother handed me their phone number and offered to show me the cascades the following day, and I was overwhelmed by their gratitude. With each step up the stairs, they creaked like an old haunted mansion. Upon my arrival to the second floor, I found my bed which was actually a simple cot with a faded pink sheet just like at Girl Scout camp. The *Lonely Liar* had once again stumbled in their description department. In desperate need of a shower, I headed to the bathrooms, where the accommodations were beyond basic. Coffee colored boards separated me from the next stall, and as I ran my hair under the cold water I looked up and saw two lizard tails peeking out from the upper corner. As I showered, the reptiles scurried around, and I got the hell out of there quickly. Skipping necessary body parts was acceptable that evening for fear of skin contact with green jungle creatures in Nicaragua. Completing my adventure, I joined up with three Aussies and an American for a much needed beer. As we drank, I found it rather exciting to speak English again but caught myself responding to the group in Spanish.

Lying in bed that night, I was woken up for the first time in a long time by howler monkeys. We were only separated by a wooden wall; it was pitch-dark, but they could be spotted through the grandiose cracks in the wall. Then the wall knocked. Knowing I was not camping at the San Diego Zoo, I imagined myself more as a member of Swiss Family Robinson that evening. Covering my head with the see-through sheet, I finally dozed back off and continued dreaming in the jungle of Finca Magdalena.

Day 7: May 31, 2008

Finca Magdalena, Nicaragua

When daylight took over at Finca Magdalena, I became Jenifer, Warrior Princess, and decided upon my entry back into the States, I would have a medal made to prove it. My trip to Finca Magdalena was conceived from the notion I would hike *Volcan Maderas*. Immediately after a healthy breakfast of glowing papayas and ripe bananas, I followed a guide out back of the farmhouse onto a heavily wooded path. Joining my group were the six Englishpersons and another couple enjoying a year around the world. One kilometer into the hike, the girlfriend of an English boy could faintly catch a breath and high-tailed it back to the farmhouse. Leaving the group, she made no excuses for not continuing up the slippery trail, stating, "This is where the two packs of cigarettes a day catch up with you." Propelling onwards, the journey up *Volcan Maderas* was the most demanding hike I had ever endured. There were many times when I wanted to quit, turn around and go back to the farmhouse. I did not care about seeing the end. Finding the strength to step forward was the most strenuous physical activity I have ever completed.

Straight up vertically for four-kilometers, it would take our group more than five hours to summit. The heavily muddy trail was exacerbated by Hurricane Alma's visit. All the way up and all the way down the volcano, I scrambled over dried-roots, tripping me through a jungle of overgrown trees and slimy moss. Before arriving at the two-kilometer halfway point, our entire group had consumed each ounce of water carefully packed that morning. We were sweating like farm animals in an August heat wave and at the halfway point debated for twenty minutes whether to turn around or push forward. Realizing I was not going to make it, the guide so generously surrendered his walking stick to me for use. Vowing never to climb anything again, including stairs or a mall escalator, I dazedly concurred to hell with the volcano and continued to move towards the top. The second half was even more unmanageable and every ten minutes I stopped to catch my breath. There are points in one's own life when one experiences something that one knows is not worth it. I have always enjoyed hiking, but on that day I did not enjoy it anymore. I hated it. I never wanted to hike again.

Arriving at the summit, I did not even know we had pulled in to the top. In order to see the view, I had to climb a tree twenty feet in the air. Standing on jelly legs and less than enthusiastic about towering upwards, I walked down to the Crater Lake instead. As my luck would have it, the day I hiked *Volcan Maderas,* swimming was not desirable because of massive rain dumped by Hurricane Alma, leaving the water murky and with poor visibility. Staying at Crater Lake only long enough to catch my breath, I began my stumble down the volcano ahead of the group, aware that my dissent would prove to be lengthier then the boys. I slipped and skidded the whole descent. Joined by the female from the round-the-world couple, it was as though I was hiking on ice. My boots were so muddy that they made no difference. Unable to obtain a grip at any point, my legs were like tennis balls as they bounced from root to root and bruised my body; blood gushed from my knees. My knees were so swollen that they were half the size of basketballs each. On the way back I could barely walk or find strength in the cold, wet ground to regain my footing. Three hours later I finally reached the plantation and grabbed a cold bottle of water and a large bottle of beer. Both were drunk with the speed of lightning.

For everyone's sake I hit the shower, where I watched two Daddy Long Legs mate while allowing the brisk, spring water to flow over my exhausted body. Tight walking the water pipes, the two spiders met each other directly above my head, and I thought 'now there is something I have never seen before.' Attempting to salvage my hiking boots, I then tried to ask if the plantation possessed a garden hose, but I only knew *jardin* and *aqua*. Somehow the lady knew what I meant, and I spent thirty minutes cleaning my boots before ordering two plates of food and enjoying a *grande* Tonia beer, since I earned them the hard way.

Day 8: June 1, 2008

Chicken busses did not run on Sunday on the Island of Ometepe. I woke up that weekend morning, feeling crippled all over, but eager to check out other parts of the island, such as the *cascades* in San Ramon. The good-natured plantation employee informed me that there were no busses. Continuously perplexed at how Central America simply shuts down on Sunday, I spent two hours trying to figure out how I was going to get back to the ferry in Moyogalpa. Without class on Monday, I would be inclined to spend one more night out on the island mainly because my body was stiff and in desperate need of rest from the hellish workout the day prior. Since my body ached all over and I really needed a walker to assist me, I spent a few hours in a hammock listening to my I-Pod and watching the sunrise while scheming up a plan. I still had the phone number from the boys who had brought me here, or I could hobble to the road and hitchhike, hoping for the best. While enjoying some *cafe con leche* and *huevos y arroz*, I observed a large group of Non-Governmental Organization workers from Central Nicaragua also staying at the hostel. Headed to the ferry around noon, I chose to wait and ride out with them. There were twenty one of us as we rode out of Finca Magdalena; I sat in the front seat with a student, who introduced himself as a landscape architect working with the NGO. Their project sounded amazing, and I could not wait to get to Ecuador and begin volunteering. Riding back to Moyogalpa, half of the NGO group decided they wanted an additional tour around the island. Stopping at the tour office, the driver ordered all of us to get out, and the price of our ride suddenly went up. I told a few members of the group this had not been part of the original deal back at Finca Magdalena, and I was really ready to get back to San Jorge. There was not much else on the island I wanted to see anyway at this late hour. Continuing to up the price now that there were less people in the van, the driver disappeared into the tour office for ten minutes, leaving us to ponder if we would catch the 2:00 PM ferry. When he sat back down behind the driver's seat, concluding he would accept the original money offer, he sped us back on the rugged, rain-soaked road to Moyogalpa. Nothing was going to get in his way, dogs included, as I watched a dog bounce off the vehicle's side and land in a shallow ravine. Closing my eyes, I said a silent prayer the van did not overturn and pummel us down the side of the island. None of it mattered pulling up to the dock, we had missed the ferry and I ended up studying Spanish on the pier for two hours before catching the last ferry home at 4:00 PM.

The 4:00 PM ferry was the last of the week-end, jam-packed with filthy backpackers and mixed with locals to throw together a putrid smell. Taking a seat near the door, I opted for fresh air instead of the melancholic view out front. When the boat pulled into San Jorge, I spotted my English friends. They had decided to visit San Juan Del Sur, so we agreed to share two cabs back to town. At the last minute, two more English girls joined up, so five of us were now in one old Toyota car, circa 1980's, along with the driver. Over the hour long ride there was a lot of lying on top of each other in the backseat, but we managed, and upon my arrival back in San Juan Del Sur, I wished them luck in their travels.

Day 9: June 2, 2008

San Juan del Sur, Nicaragua

It was official. I was a semi-permanent resident of the country after retrieving a *biblioteca* card and checking out two books, including *My First 500 Spanish Words* to aide me in learning my colors and parts of the body. There was also a new student in school that day; in addition, she took up residency at my home. Quite farther along the in Spanish language, she taught me to sing 'head shoulders, knees and toes, knees and toes' in Spanish leading me to believe that I could be a doctor if the case arose. Today was a difficult day for me because I got a new teacher and she attempted to teach me adjectives and pronouns, but they didn't click and just led to frustration. Too much information was coming my way, and I began to shut down. Day dreaming in the middle of class, I lost focus many times and began to believe I was too old to go back to school.

Day 10: June 3, 2008

San Juan del Sur, Nicaragua

My new teacher was named Ana and together we spent an hour on adjectives today before I almost broke down in tears.

Then I found out it's because her chart was a little off then suddenly it clicked a little better. For our afternoon activity we went to *Playa Maderas,* right outside of San Juan del Sur and my new class/housemate, Jessica, surfed. Since I was not a big fan I took in the view and watched as the *lluvia* came down on the surfers.

By now I was pretty much over this town and ready to move on...not being a surfer I don't think the town has much to offer me anymore. After arriving back home we had a great dinner of *mas tipo gallo de pinto*, but I had taken notice that my body was changing. Extra weight on my hips and buttocks was taking shape, even though I did exercises in my room and continued practicing counting in Spanish every night.

Day 11: June 4, 2008

San Juan Del Sur, Nicaragua

It is now mid-second week of my stay in San Juan del Sur. I ran into the English boys from Ometepe. Offering up a reference to the *Latin American Spanish School,* they decided to attend as well. Their friendly attitude was a welcome addition to the school. Later the same day the sky blackened with soot as a car caught fire at the end of the street near the San Juan Del Sur *biblioteca*. Sirens whaling, the *bomberos* came, and an impressive explosion was avoided. When my new housemate and I joined our family for lunch, we were surprised with pasta, which I did not even know they made in Central America. Living with a typical Nicaraguan family, I experienced numerous different meals, mostly mixed with *gallos de pintos*. For lunch one day we had *pescado sopa* and my housemate grabbed me to scream, "Oh' My God! There is a whole fish in my soup!" Busy looking at wedding photos donning the walls, I said, "Ok, just take it one sip at a time." Five minutes later I realized it was hard to concentrate while two fish eyes are staring at me and my host mom is asking *"Te gusta sopa?"* Together, we tackled the snapper, bone by bone, placing each scale on our side plate. It was moments like that I was eternally grateful I received all my Hepatitis shots.

Day 12: June 5, 2008

San Juan del Sur, Nicaragua

Roosters crowed at 3:10 AM every day, just to be exact. But tomorrow was the last day I would have to hear them in San Juan del Sur. Since I was up, I headed to the *mercado* to observe the early shoppers and work on my Spanish. Sitting by the little *comida* and *carniceria*, I studied and sipped rich, dark coffee as the day commenced. When I paid my bill, it was only twenty-five cents, and I thought I heard her incorrectly. So used to shelling out over four-dollars for coffee in the States, I was amazed at how cheap everything was there. Back at my host-home, breakfast consisted of a hearty helping of eggs and rice. Then morning class was cut short as Mother's Day festivities had been re-scheduled from Hurricane Alma's visit. During class my professor and I did take a field trip to the market and around town to practice Spanish, which helped me a great deal. My professor asked me to accompany her to the elementary school to listen as her daughter presented a poem, so I joined them and watched as the children of San Juan Del Sur read and danced. Dressed in their traditional blue bottoms and white tops, the children marched out in their uniforms, while mothers donned elegant dresses and high heels.

My final evening in San Juan Del Sur, I assisted in the kitchen. After two weeks of asking *"Como Puede Ayudarte,"* I was allowed to help the family make fried plantains and cabbage salad. The kitchen was located adjacent to the main house, the stove lit by logs and fire. Wandering underneath my feet was the house cat; I swatted him away not relishing the idea that a feline preyed near my dinner. Later in the evening little Maria needed help with homework, and I assisted her. It was then that I realized she was placed in a primary class, even though she was ten years old. Relaxing in their rocking chairs, no one at the house was anxious to help her, and half the time school was canceled anyway. Her school supplies consisted of a few short, broken pencils and no erasers, leaving me to fear she would just grow up illiterate. Even more upsetting was the attention the family paid to all of their sons, but simply forgot this little girl.

Day 13: June 6, 2008

San Juan del Sur, Nicaragua to Playa del Coco, Costa Rica

Graduation Day!

Leaving San Juan Del Sur, I said goodbye to everyone and headed to catch the noon bus. Unusual for Central America, it was half empty, and I was able to take the front seat with plenty of room for me and my backpack. I was on the first bus out of that town; after two weeks I needed a change of pace. Noon was the perfect time to catch the bus; riding along were only school kids who hopped off soon. The bus costs fifteen *Córdoba's* or around seventy-five cents, but all I had left was a one-hundred-dollar *Córdoba*. Asking for change in Central America was like requesting extra time on one's curfew while in high school; it never came. Shopkeepers consistently tell you they do not have it, leaving you with large bills or no product. This meant I was always walking around with what denomination that shot out of the automatic teller machine. On all busses in Central America there was a driver and a money handler. Forced to hand the money handler my one-hundred-dollar *Córdoba*, he viewed me as a piggy-bank. He walked towards the back of the bus with my money, and after forty minutes I finally tapped him on the back and asked for my change. Not being too pushy since he carried a machete in his back pocket, there was plenty to be uncomfortable about, but I did need my money. This was also the time I needed to be let off back at the middle of the nowhere intersection, so he dropped the remaining *Córdoba's* in my hand as he asked *"A Donde Va?"* Knowing I could not pronounce the intersection, I held up a piece of paper with Spanish scribbled on it, and he kindly helped me step off with my backpack. *"Buenas Suerte"* he yelled and pointed me across the street as the bus drove off. Waiting under a tree with the locals, I nervously hoped I was in the correct spot when I recognized a bus with the words *Penas Blancas* painted on the front. Handing my backpack off to two guys riding on the roof, I watched all my belongings disappear into an obscure field of chicken coops and massive bags of rice. Climbing in through the back door, I leaned against the metal rails receiving painful cerebral bruises each time we hit a bump. Two seats up, a man offered me his seat and I was ecstatic to enjoy the ride from the café-brown covered seats.

Exiting the bus at Penas Blancas, I spotted another American male and asked if he would like to cross together. Nearby there were Latino eyes all over and I knew it was best to cross into Costa Rica sans solo. Twenty steps later I recognized Penas Blancas to be the most confusing border crossing ever. There were no signs directing one from Nicaragua to Costa Rica, just mobs of men pestering me for money-including directions or the use of a pen to fill out your customs form. In Penas Blancas, one's goal was to reach a dilapidated, white building; however, prior to one's arrival there was a man requesting one-dollar to leave Nicaragua. I still did not understand why I must pay to leave countries willingly and mistrusted where the hell the money was going. (Surely not to the roads, education, or healthcare systems.) Next, I walked through what appeared to be a one-kilometer maze of a truck weighing station towards Costa Rica, where I was forced to produce my passport to an official lazily positioned beneath a giant, worn tarp. While simultaneously attempting not to be run over by one-thousand pound big rigs and fishing out my passport from my money belt, I crisscrossed through the muddy banks in whichever country I was in called a road. Pointing me two-hundred feet into a separate building, it was necessary to show my passport again before paying the nominal two-dollar entrance fee and gaining another receipt of some kind. It was highly recommended not to lose one's Costa Rican entry receipt, for this could make exiting the country one of the most difficult exits in Central America. Finally, I waited for forty-five minutes to catch a bus because, of course, there was not one arriving when the *Lonely Planet* stated. When the bus pulled in, it was the typical old Greyhound with no air-conditioning, but I did gain a seat, so I got comfortable for the two hour ride to Liberia, Costa Rica. Twenty minutes down the road Costa Rican Police officials stopped our bus and demanded our passports. Nerves shot to hell, I had never been scrutinized so much to enter or exit a country. I had shown my passport more in an hour then in two months total. Once the *policía* exited, I looked out the window in an attempt to regain my composure. Costa Rica's countryside was so green; it was as if a leprechaun dumped a bunch of fairy dust upon it. Hillsides shone in shades of lush emerald and trees popped as though it was the first day of spring.

When the bus pulled into Liberia, it was six minutes late for my connecting bus to Playa Del Coco. Running throughout the terminal with my two oversized packs, I glanced at my watch and realized I would be forced to sit for two-and-a-half-hours until the last bus of the day headed out. Taking up space on a simple blue bench, I tied my giant pack around my legs and my Camelback around my chest to fend off pick-pocketers. Nervously, I pulled out a book to pass the time, but was unable to concentrate on reading while getting isolated stares from everyone in the station. Surrounded by Costa Ricans, my pulse quickened each time a vendor neared me offering pirated CD's or phony silver bracelets.

When I stepped onto the bus, I took up space next to a young *Tico* dressed in an Oakland Raiders jersey, who, I swore, introduced himself to me as Windmill. Since he just had his molars taken out, I only made him repeat it twice and decided Windmill it was. Knowing zero English, he was a little chatter bug from Liberia to Playa del Coco, but I was really not in the mood to be social, since I had been traveling for six hours and had not eaten since breakfast. Gabbing the whole hour to Playa Del Coco, the Spanish was good practice. But I was tired and hungry and considering his dental work situation, I had to lean in every time to fully comprehend his relentless questioning, which included the three most popular questions in Central America, *Tu eres casada, Tu eres novio, Tu eres hijos?* When locals heard I was not married, no boyfriend, and without kids, they stared at me in astonishment and shouted to the rafters *Por Que, Por Que?* These were the first three questions out of anyone's mouth in Central America, especially pinpointing where my *hijos* were. There was no need for a husband, just where were my kids.

Large drops of rain had begun to clop down on the road. This evoked short visibility, so as we rolled into Playa Del Coco, I peered down the streets attempting to follow my directions from another Couchsurfer. Any excuse to assist a *Gringa,* two sketchy looking guys attempted to walk me to my next Couchsurfer's house. Not in the mood to get raped, I fended off their advances, and with a quick *mucho gusto*, I ducked into a restaurant and spent several minutes waiting for them to leave the area. It was at that time that I realized if there was one country I was going to need pepper spray in, it would be Costa Rica. With the influx of *Gringa's* coming to visit, they were an aggressive group of *Ticos*, but I was not there to bring one home in my backpack. Looking for a gravel road to lead me towards a Couchsurfer's home, I continued down a path that was now paved, but was exactly how she described it in her email. Leading me one-kilometer out of town, the road shined as large drops of rain continued to pour down. Passing by me were numerous *Ticos* commenting on my body, and my fingers wrapped around my pepper spray with desperation. It was late and dark; I picked up the pace and crossed the road where I discovered the privately owned complex. Passing by the homes, a dark-skinned guard popped out from behind a heavy bush and startled me, so when I showed up at the Couchsurfer's condominium, I was a wet and frightened mess of backpacker. Apologetic for the river I drug in, she laughed and welcomed me in, ushering me into the bathroom where I received my first hot shower in two weeks.

Day 14-June 7, 2008-

Playa Del Coco, Costa Rica/Playa Hermosa, Costa Rica

The next morning I woke up and had a nice, warm breakfast of oatmeal that I backpacked down to Central America. I was grateful to be in ´civilization´ where I had access to a microwave. The woman I was Couchsurfing with announced she was going diving in Playa Hermosa, located about nine-kilometers north of Playa Del Coco. I headed off with her and enjoyed a day to myself at the beach while she dove with starfish. After two weeks of Spanish class, that first day in Costa Rica was spent doing absolutely nothing but sitting on a secluded beach and finally reading my book. Scanning the beach, there was no possible way for me to take a swim as the dangers of leaving my valuables on the beach were too great. After returning to Playa Del Coco, my host showed me a satisfying *soda,* where we had *casados.* It was not hard to decide on the chicken, black beans, rice and pasta salad. Less than five-dollars, I wiped my plate clean as the food was exemplary. Closing out the day, I enjoyed a swim at her pool, where eight tourists from Kentucky splashed along. In Costa Rica on vacation, they found themselves located in the condo next to my host. An invitation to hang out with them by the pool led to an early-evening visit by the guards. Pointing to the pool rules, which were all in Spanish, the guard informed us we were bustling with illegal condominium activity. Being the only member of the group that spoke any Spanish, I translated, and, basically all the rules were being broken, like drinking, horseplay, and singing. After saying goodnight, I peaked at my watch and realized it was only 8:48 PM and thought the guards needed to chill out. We were all on vacation.

Day 15: June 8, 2008

Playa del Coco, Costa Rica

Waking up the next morning I tried to read by the pool and my Couchsurfing host had her front gate locked up like Fort Knox. Conversing with the Kentuckians through the locked bars, the host miniature Chihuahua snarled at me like he was a German Sheppard, while donning his pink collar, before finally I was unlocked from the prison I had found myself in. I ended up heading to the beach with the Kentucky folks, where we wallowed in the sun, before returning back to Playa Del Coco and I led them to the local ice cream store...of course. Later, as a rainy season afternoon storm visited the area, we hung out in the pool while the drops beat down on us. With the sun shining and tropical birds chirping, we experienced the rainstorm from the confines of the pool; swimming underwater I could feel the drops with each stroke I took.

Day 16: June 9, 2008

Playa del Coco, Costa Rica to Volcan Arenal, Costa Rica

By day sixteen of my trip, I looked as though I had chicken pox all over my body from all the ants and mosquito bites. The thirty and forty proof DEET was not working, and I was thinking I should have bought the one-hundred proof Leaving Playa Del Coco, the Kentucky group offered to let me ride with them to Volcan Arenal. At night the lava and incandescent lights draw tourists from around the region in hopes to view the spectacular sight. Surrounding the volcano is Lake Arenal, arguably the most beautiful place in Costa Rica. Heading down the narrow highway, our group was separated in two rental cars. The guys had walkie talkies to keep in contact with each other, and it reminded me of my guy friends back in the States as they horse played over the next three and a half hours. Bumping through pot holes, I marveled at how rough the roads in Costa Rica were, considering the massive amounts of tourism seen by the country. Yet, the infrastructure was as lacking as Honduras or Guatemala. Coming around *Lago Arenal*, the overlook provided fantastic photo opportunities although I did not believe it to be the most spectacular site I had seen in Central America. Costa Rica was beautiful, but definitely not the most stunning my eyes had beheld in the Latin American region. Definitely overpriced, there were sites more enchanting at a cheaper rate, but the tourist industry arrived in Costa Rica first. I hiked into a trail near the Volcan Arenal Observatory and stumbled upon a waterfall. Finding the waterfall average, it was not the most alluring I had seen. Close by I passed the volcano, a blanket of jet-black coal cloaked in a cotton ball cloud forest. Massive by all accounts, I hoped to catch a glimpse of the fiery-red coals later that evening.

Afterwards, I was prepared to hike the fifteen-kilometers back into La Fortuna, where I was planning to bunker down for the night. Costa Rica was well beyond my budget allotment, and I was cutting corners anyway possible. The lodge wanted twenty-dollars for a shuttle into town, and I refused to surrender to their inflated prices. As I was getting ready to begin my adventure, a car set out to depart the parking lot. I asked them *"A Donde Va?"* They responded La Fortuna and told me to hop in. Waving a gracious thank you to the Kentucky group, I transferred my backpack into the car and accepted the ride into La Fortuna. Spotting a hostel aptly named *Gringo Pete's,* which was a big purple house on the edge of La Fortuna, I quickly asked if they had any beds. The young *Tica* laughed as there was only one other girl taking up space in the hostel that night since it was the beginning of Costa Rica's off season. For $4/US that night, I had a room basically to myself, free Costa Rican morning coffee, a backyard with a BBQ, a library and reading area, and a nice big kitchen. Walls were adorned with any information necessary to travel between Panama and Nicaragua, and I scanned them for awhile searching for any piece of assistance. I was lured by the many outdoor activities in La Fortuna, including bungee jumping and river rafting; however, their asking prices were well beyond my price range. I had heard that one do-not-miss opportunity in La Fortuna was the Baldi Hot Springs, so I went ahead and bought a ticket for the spa-like relaxation point and then walked to lunch at *Soda El Rio*. *Sodas* were a common spot for grabbing standard dishes throughout Costa Rica and kept me on my twenty-eight-dollar a day budget. *Soda El Rio* was a quaint little place and for about five-dollars, I chowed down on a Thanksgiving feast of a *casado*, carne, rice, beans, banana, and salad. Full and ready to pop through my pants, the waiter brought me a complimentary *arroz con leche for* dessert. Already worried about not fitting into my clothes, I decided to savor every bite and walk it off on the four-kilometers leading out to the hot springs. As I began walking, I noticed the road was a little too dangerous with the Central American drivers, minus the fact the roads were missing sidewalks. Waving down a taxi cab, I attempted to bargain for the remaining two-kilometers, yet his asking price was above any backpacker's budget. Pulling over at an ATV business, I asked the ATV operator if he was headed my way. He said he was and would be happy to give me a lift, so I hopped in. Reluctant to hitchhike back in Belize, I was now a true adventure-seeker and knew that accepting rides from strangers was a must of the backpacking world. There were plenty of other opportunities for me to be harmed on my trip; least of all, I expected it to happen in a strange vehicle.

Once at the Hot Springs, I was in heaven. Entering, there were strange and disapproving looks sent my way. Other customers possessed clean clothes and groomed hair; I walked in wearing a grimy baseball cap, TEVA flip flops, and my much-used Appalachian State University t-shirt. The smell on that alone needed to be isolated in a canister. I had not expected the hot springs to be at such a high standard. Home to sixteen hot springs, several cold ones, a spa to receive massages and facials, and a sauna, the Baldi Hot Springs were comparable to an impressive sight I may stumble upon in the States. I found the entire area rather exciting and stayed for eight hours. Towards the back of the property was a water slide, waterfalls, and full bar, all within view of *Volcan Arenal.* Within minutes of my arrival, a rainstorm hit and trickled down on me as I took shelter in the one-hundred and four degree pool. Surrounded by lush green landscape and giant blooming flowers, my body enjoyed the warmth of the pool as my head became covered with raindrops. An amazing experience, I never wanted to leave the confines within where I lay. That afternoon in Costa Rica would turn out to be my favorite in the country. Without the hassle of *Ticos* lurking behind my every step, I was compelled never to leave. Visiting a pool near the volcano, it was the perfect spot to watch the sunset. Three steps in to the pool, it immediately dropped off to ten feet, and I plunged in as water overtook my body, and I grasped for footing. None was to be found. Gasping for air, I dog-paddled towards the stairs and reached for the hand rail. My Camelback was heavy with spring water; ripping open the zipper I found my *Lonely Planet* and journal bleeding into each other. As I went to take a picture, my camera suddenly did not power on. Promised to be water and shock proof, after fidgeting with it for a while, I concluded it was broken. Despite my fatal attempts to salvage the camera, the remainder of the evening would be spent online with warranties and emails.

I would spend an entire day in La Fortuna, Costa Rica, struggling to ship my camera back to California. First, I headed to the Internet café where I was unable to print out the necessary shipping documents since the computer did not have the latest Adobe Acrobat updates. Next, I attempted to go all over La Fortuna looking for packaging supplies, but was offered nothing better than a large brown non-padded envelope. Finally, I did find a UPS Outlet after two hours of looking around the small town of only seven-thousand people, but they required one-hundred-and-fifteen-dollars to ship it to the United States California Olympus Center even though UPS offers discounts to Olympus customers. All of this and I still needed a camera, so I decided to head into the capital of San Jose tomorrow even though I had sworn not to visit there.

Day 17-June 10, 2008

La Fortuna, Costa Rica to San Jose, Costa Rica

Stepping up to the San Jose bus, I handed US dollars to the driver. To that point in Costa Rica, I had paid in US dollars and received US dollars back. I was nothing but surprised when the bus driver refused to take US dollars for the bus ride. Sending me on my way to the supermarket for change, I was forced to make a purchase; upon my return the bus had jetted out of town. *"A Donde Va,"* said the taxi driver behind me, and I thought to myself I wanted no part of him. But the next bus did not leave for two more hours. Striking a deal with the taxi driver, he agreed to catch up with the bus; yet it took him fifteen minutes, leading me to believe the bus jetted out of La Fortuna as soon as I turned around. Along the drive, the taxi driver flipped out his cell phone to make contact with the bus and request them to stop, obviously telling me the refusal of dollars was a scam they use on backpackers all the time. Upon catching up to the bus, the taxi driver demanded more money. Handing him less then half for being a crook, while he shouted obscenities at me, I boarded the bus

An alligator lounging on the New River during the boat tour to Lamanai.

Caracol Mayan site.

Lago Peten Itza, located in El Remate, Guatemala near Tikal.

Tikal

The author clowning around at a festival in Copan, Honduras.

The author attending a cockfight in Copan, Honduras.

The author climbing Volcan Pacaya near Antigua, Guatemala.

The author climbing Volcan Pacaya near Antigua, Guatemala.

A young child dressed for Semana Santa celebrations in
Antigua, Guatemala.

Tourists and locals assist in preparing the streets of Antigua, Guatemala for Semana Santa celebrations.

The author snorkeling with stingrays near Caye Caulker, Belize.

The author hiking up Volcan Maderas, located on the
Island of Ometepe, Nicaragua.

Grounds of Finca Magdalena, located on the Island of
Ometepe, Nicaragua.

The desolate beaches of Playa Blanca, Colombia.

Church in Cartagena, Colombia.

Castillo de San Felipe de Barajas,
Cartagena, Colombia.

Basílica del Voto Nacional, Quito, Ecuador.

Inside view of the author's housing accommodations in Guayama, Ecuador.

Author's housing accommodations in Guayama, Ecuador.

The author at the entrance to Actun Tunichil Muknal near
San Ignacio, Belize.

and cursed myself at being ripped off. The bus ride between La Fortuna and San Jose was just as popular for thieves, so I sat in the back and kept my bag latched to me, finally arriving in San Jose four hours later. There were just as many crooks in the capital waiting on every corner including the taxi driver who brought me to the hostel. With the number of prostitutes and drug dealers lining the trash-littered streets near the San Jose bus station, there was no way I could walk in that part of town without getting mugged or something worse. Looking to keep a low profile for an even lower amount of time in San Jose, I dressed in long brown dry-pants, hiking boots, a long-sleeve plain black t-shirt, and my baseball cap. Plain. That was how I wanted it. No attention on me.

After arriving at the Tranquillo Backpackers Hostel, I immediately headed three blocks down the street to a Radio Shack where their digital camera selection was that of four cameras total, three consisting of the same brand. None to my satisfaction, I spent the next hour shopping at four different stores, my complacency level at a zero. Since I had just purchased two new memory sticks for the trip, it would have been nice to find something compatible, but apparently Olympus chose not to sell anything in Costa Rica. Watching men push anything and everything on the streets, I gave up looking for a new camera and headed back to my hostel as the rain started pouring down. Barricading myself in the hostel, with a storm raging and no interest in seeing San Jose, I spent the evening shopping online for a camera, despite the fact I could not have it sent to Costa Rica because of import fees and taxes. The magic travel stories I had heard of this country were yet to be seen.

Day 18: June 11, 2008

San José, Costa Rica to Bocas del Toro, Panama

There were no roosters in San Jose, but ducks quacked in the middle of the city and woke me long before the sky cleared of darkness, promptly at 5:30 AM. Rising out of bed I took the time to catch up on the computer before enjoying complimentary pancakes and coffee provided by the hostel. As I enjoyed my coffee, I realized that the *Lonely Liar* misquoted yet another bus time, and my ride to the Panama border left San Jose at 9:00 AM, not 10:00 AM. Fleeing frantically onto the street, I attempted to hail a cab to the bus station. Being morning rush hour in San Jose, I watched as hordes of taxis drove past me already full. Ones that did stop requested twice the normal amount to take me to the bus station. When I finally arrived I found out I needed to be at the opposite bus station across town. I had fourteen minutes to get three hundred meters, which sounded close but in San Jose morning traffic was not. I was compelled to walk the distance until the locals directed me that the area was far too dangerous. Stepping into another taxi, I raced through San Jose morning traffic, where I threw my money at the driver and sprinted onto the bus as my watch switched to 9:00 AM. Half empty, since it was off-season, I sprawled across two seats, one for me and one for my backpack. It would be an eight-hour journey to Bocas del Toro, Panama, so as the bus drove off I attempted to brush up on Spanish. Yet, tired from my early morning duck alarm, I quickly dozed off, and when I opened my eyes, an impressive sight of the Caribbean Sea was on my left. My eyes met miles of pristine white beaches lined with hundreds of palm trees swaying in the breeze.

As one drives the Pan-American Highway from San Jose towards Sixaola, the road flattens and to the West is lined with hundreds of tall, lanky palms bordering the Caribbean ocean. From the bus window the sea looked calm, and I noticed gentle waves rolling in every few seconds. The beauty of the beach was unmistakable, and the beaches were so isolated as if they were waiting for a beer commercial to be filmed. The bus continued to head South to Sixaola, and slowly the beach faded away only to be replaced by thousands of acres of banana fields. My mind could only compare it to Nebraska as one drives through the numerous corn fields set to feed millions of people. The entire Southeast corner of Costa Rica and North Eastern slice of Panama were covered in banana fields. Most of the men on my bus dressed in blue polo shirts with the word *'Chiquita'* stitched on them, as the bus headed to a town called Changuinola, headquarters of the Chiriquí Land Company, the very same people that bring the Chiquita bananas. Changuinola is where I was heading to connect to a ferry for Bocas del Toro. It was the center of the banana trade, but I did not expect to find much more there. As it turned out, the factory was huge and the port even bigger. It made the San Diego port look like small potatoes.

When we pulled into the border of Costa Rica and Panama, I walked briskly over to the Costa Rica building. There was a group of Swiss girls out front, sitting down on the concrete savoring tropical fruit, their faces covered with exhaust after a long day of traveling. I stepped over them and presented the Costa Rican official my receipt for when I entered the country just a few days back. He stamped my passport, and I left. A flash ran through my mind about why they had not asked me to pay the five-dollar tourism entry fee into Panama, but I thought maybe they had just waived it. I headed back to the bus and used up my last thirty-cents in Costa Rican colons to purchase some juicy papaya and ate it as the juice stained my Appalachian State t-shirt. It was then that the bus driver asked me if I also crossed the bridge over to Panama.

"I thought this was Panama," I said to him.

"No, you must go across the bridge," he advised me in Spanish.

It was then that I turned around and noticed the half-mile wooden bridge which looked as though it came out of an Indiana Jones movie. Beginning to head across, the creaky planks were sporadic and shook with each step I took. There was a river underneath, no doubt filled with crocodiles and man-eating fish. Balancing myself on the ancient bridge, I wiped drips of sweat from my nose as this region of the world was so hot; I had noticed that it only got hotter with each country. I was loaded down with my two backpacks and assumed that I appeared to the locals that I was going to tumble off like a child's block formation at any moment. To the sides of the bridge was nothing but chicken wire to keep one from jumping. Pedestrians shared the bridge with busses and freight trucks, so it was necessary for me to traffic across the contraption in a rapid manner or else be flattened like a pancake by a motor vehicle.

After safely crossing the bridge, I reached the Panama border crossing. There were so many men; most of them had forgotten to wear their shirts that day and were forcing themselves into a small window labeled 'Visas.' I wedged myself between them to the front of the line where the woman eyed me with sorrow and pointed to a window next door. There did not appear to be anyone working, and I questioned myself as to whether or not I understood her Spanish correctly and was at the right place. A man behind me yelled and I turned to see a Panama border official running over to assist me. He asked me to please enter his office, and I followed him inside where he invited me to sit down on the simple, metal chair, so I did as instructed and watched with interest as he wrote my name in a book, along with my passport number.

He wanted to know if I was traveling alone. Yes, I was traveling alone; no, I did not have a husband, a boyfriend or any children. Compelled to snap back to him "Is that a problem," instead I choose to keep quiet so I could make it into Panama alive. "Why are you traveling alone and to where are you going," he questioned me in Spanish. This again...I was really getting tired of everyone in Latin America trying to marry me off. Could a single woman not travel alone? Upset by his questions I watched as he laid my passport down and leaned back in his chair nonchalantly, genuinely interested in why there was no one accompanying me. Looking him square in the eye I said, "I have no husband. It is just me." Shaking his head, the man requested my five-dollars to enter Panama before directing me back outside.

To return to the bus, I needed to head back across the Indiana Jones bridge. Trotting as fast as I could with my heavy travel weight, halfway back, my bus was already driving towards me. Back on the Costa Rican side, a ferocious taxi driver had been trying to sell me on the fact that the bus would not make it to the town of Changuinola for the last *lancha* of the day. Fed up with conspiring *Ticos,* I did not buy his story, so I was back on the bus. Tapping the driver on his shoulder, I nervously asked how much longer to Changuinola, praying I had gambled correctly. He told me we would make it there by 4:30 PM; the last *lancha* was scheduled to leave at 6:00 PM.

When I got to Changuinola, I was bombarded by greedy taxi drivers. Before I could even step off the bus, they were reaching their hands out, offering to drive me to the *lancha* for a great price. The men positioned their hands around my waist, aiming for my backpack in order to place it in their cars. My attempts at negotiation with them were feeble at best, and I finally decided to hop into a *collectivo*. Speaking Spanish with the driver, I responded in English by mistake, and he ended up talking to me the whole way because he wanted to practice his English. It was getting tiresome seeking out Spanish speakers in Costa Rica and on the Panama border; everyone wanted to speak English, what they referred to as the 'Universal Language.' My reasons for returning to Latin America were to become fluent in Spanish, yet it was becoming impossible since everyone wanted to learn English.

The taxi drove me to Almirante where I bought a ticket for a little speed boat *lancha*. Wandering exactly where in the hell I was, I took a seat on a log bench while noticing many pairs of dark Panamanian eyes watching me. All alone on the platform, I secretly wished there were other white faces around to remove the attention from me. As I waited, a sixteen-year-old Costa Rican boy sat down and asked if I had a boyfriend as he looked suspiciously at my luggage. While keeping two hands on my bags so he could not steal them, I broke the news to him that in the United States I did not date sixteen-year-old boys, and he was not coming home with me. Continuing with the questions, he asked, *"A Donde Va"* and I watched as he and his little friends were way too willing to help with my backpack. Tired of making conversation, I tossed the pack on my back and loaded onto the boat solo.

As we pulled away, there were hundreds of tiny islands, surrounded by thick greenery, dotting the coast of Panama. With no digital camera, I attempted to shoot the images through a disposable device I had packed as a reserve. Soon, we pulled up to a canoe in the middle of the ocean where we handed over two large packages of rice before the canoe paddled away. The *Lonely Planet* read that one can canoe between the islands, but since it took the speedboat forty-five minutes to get there, who knew how long it would take me in a damn canoe. After pulling into Bocas del Toro, I headed to the Mondo Taitu hostel which was a big tree house full of fun, including a bar that had fifty-cent beer and a complimentary pancake breakfast, plus other free perks like movies, bikes and beach toys. I put my backpack down and in walked Jeffrey, a guy I had met back in Caye Caulker; we had played trivia night together. Both traveling separately for several months, I could not comprehend what a small world it really was!

Since leaving San Jose almost ten hours prior, by that time I was in desperate need for a shower. But a glitch in the Bocas del Toro water department meant no water flowed through the hostel for another hour. Joining my new hostel friends, I enjoyed some fifty-cent beers before feeling the touch of cold water ripple on top of me. After the sun went down, I stepped into a one-dollar boat carrying passengers to Isla Carenero, a quick shot across the Caribbean Sea from Bocas Del Toro. Located on Isla Carenero was the Aqua Bar where it was Ladies Night. In Panama that meant ladies drank for free, not simply a reduced price. The Aqua Bar was mounted on a platform over the ocean; with a pool in the middle of the bar, people were encouraged to jump in, finding themselves drenched in ocean water. As the night wore on and the free drinks flowed, I witnessed girls and guys stripping down nude, climbing the ladder and flipping off Olympic style. Spirits were high, and we danced until the rain started. The first of many nights I would spend in Panama, my mind was only focused on how freeing it was to dance on an island in the middle of the Caribbean!

Day 19-June 12, 2008

Bocas Del Toro, Panama

Finishing breakfast, hostel-mate, Tom, suggested some of us hike La Gruta, a cavern on the Western side of Bocas Del Toro Island. I was totally up for the challenge and was inspired to explore the cave since I had read about it before coming to the island. We grabbed two hostel mates and began the eight-kilometer journey. As we attempted to bargain with taxis, drivers shook their heads at us and barked back in Spanish that twenty-dollars was the asking price. Refusing to give in to their demands, we logged in exercise until hailing a *collectivo* to take us the remaining way for one-dollar each. I enjoyed the drive by peering through the twenty foot tall jungle on either side of the road; it was simply too bad I had forgotten to pack my machete. Turning out to be much farther than eight-kilometers, the distance stretched on ascending far into a wandering forest. Seeing no other people throughout our trip, I gathered we were being taken into no-man's-land. Once stopped, a worn, brown sign read La Gruta, and a long path directed us to a statue of the Virgin Mary, who marked the entrance to the cave. There was a small, old Panamanian woman washing her laundry at the entrance. Lifting her head she pointed to us and announced in Spanish that we must pay her one-dollar to enter. Suspicious, I questioned where the money was going. She let it be known the money went to maintaining the cave, but I concluded it went into her pocket. And what was she going to do if we did not pay her?

As we began to enter the cave, I was ecstatic I packed my PETZL head lamp. My feet were going into waist high water, possessing a murky, brown color. I could not see any visibility in the water. Fearing there were snakes below, my heart beat quickened when all of a sudden, a bat flew by my head, and I screamed like the girl I am. Looking upwards, there were thousands of bats overhead, and many of them were flying past me in no particular direction. My pulse was beating at a pace that was probably going to kill me. I realized that I was going to die there, and the Department of State was going to say "we told you not to go hiking with bats in Panama." Each step led my foot into unknown territory, grasping for footing in a maze of gloppy mud and filth. As we spotted the exit, on the right was the world's largest spider, savoring what appeared to be a mosquito, and I winced at the thought of being bit by some unknown species of arachnoids and dying in a Panamanian jungle. Glancing at the roof, I flinched as hundreds of jet black bats were clumped together on the ceiling. Knowing my PETZL lamp was going to wake them, I got the hell out of there while the boys laughed at me and Tom yelled "Quitter!" Call me a coward, I did not care, I was going to live to see another day. Down another path of aggressive jungle leaves and killer ants was a second cave, which I suspiciously started entering when I heard the boys let out a blood-curling scream. Massive bats exited the cave. Forget it! I was out of there as the second girl replied something touched her foot, and I moved at lightning speed. While the boys continued their mission, a case of diarrhea suddenly hit me hard. Carrying no toilet paper and with no bathroom in sight, I strongly attempted to hold it in before being forced to squat in the wilderness. I waited for the diarrhea to finish as massive ants entered my Teva's and feasted on my feet. Hearing the boys exit the cave, I pulled up my pants and could smell the unpleasantness; hoping it did not fill the air. At the exit to La Gruta the road was deserted, and we were forced to wait twenty minutes for a taxi. I climbed in clinching my legs tightly together and returned to the hostel to scrub all the bats and poop off me. Standing in the shower, I reflected on the day and conceived that three-dollars is apparently what I thought my life was worth.

Day 20-June 13, 2008

When I was growing up, my brother and sister said I could take a job at the IHOP one day because I made awesome pancakes. Some things never change as those skills came in handy for all my breakfast meals at Mondo Taitu. My pancakes were the envy of everyone else's in the hostel kitchen, and I spent time showing the importance of thick batter to backpackers from around the world. Following breakfast the second morning, I joined up with two Americans, to proceed out on our boat and snorkel trip. We met up with Captain Leroy, but not before one American insisted we grab some Panamanian beer to help our cruise endeavors around the islands. It was only 9:30 AM, but the sun was shining and we were all on vacation, so celebrations called for a morning toast. Leaning into the wind and holding onto our beers, we rode off through the hot sunshine feeling the spray of saltwater as the boat chopped the waves. Mounting swells caused our beers to bubble over and more than one passenger to receive a chipped tooth. Whipping around, I stretched my legs out for more comfort and padded my rear with my hot pink beach towel. Captain Leroy laughed as he sailed us to Dolphin Cove where we witnessed the dolphins play and swim around the mangroves. Spotting only a few, we were fascinated as a herd joined up and we urged Captain Leroy to stick around a while longer. Next, we sailed over to Cayo Crawl for some snorkeling and what appeared to be a make shift restaurant on stilts. Leaping into the sea, there was a strong current, and I spotted hundreds of tiny jellyfish urging me to climb back out. Afraid of being stung, the novelty of snorkeling wore off fast. Fighting my way through the intense current, on this occasion I found my swimming skills mediocre and pushed my body to its limit just to reach the deck. I watched as another swimmer had to be brought in on a motor boat and chose to lounge around on the stilts and two by fours until our departure.

When we drove off, Captain Leroy led us to a secluded spot he enjoyed, and I bounded into the water again. Snorkeling there I witnessed the most beautiful coral I had ever seen. The colors were so alive; images of bright hot pink, lime green, ensembles of blue and orange. Amazing coral dressed the floor of the ocean while along strolled stingrays and turtles. Everything was so alive! I was lured to swim farther out, but inevitably I had no partner or guide and turned around when darkness took over and the perimeter fogged up. Ending the day, Captain Leroy piloted the boat onward to Red Frog Beach where I was met by a young boy running up thrusting a *rana roja*, or strawberry poison dart frog, at me. He wanted me to touch it, but I remembered reading about them at the aquarium and brushed past him. At Red Frog Beach, there was a little bar that looked like Tom Cruise should be working there in *Cocktail,* and nothing else. An impressive sight, the waves were huge and I jumped in to bodysurf. Crashing down on me, the massive waves sent my body crumbling into the sand, leaving me half nude and searching for my bikini top. Realizing I was topless, I searched for the petite piece of fabric and spotted it floating nearby. Securing it tightly into place, I was lured to attempt the wave again and bodysurfed until I had no more energy. I was compelled never to leave paradise, but as the afternoon rain came in, Captain Leroy communicated the need to return to Bocas del Toro.

The last night at Mondo Taitu, a theme party was put in place. Taking advantage of the hostel's costume closet, in no time I transformed into a pirate. No vacancy in sight and happy hour flowing, Mondo Taitu melted into a drunken haven for young backpackers and Peace Corps volunteers on weekend getaways. Further into the evening some friends and I ordered a mango-fruit hookah. As we smoked, strangers became friends and I breathed in, imagining a life on Bocas del Toro where everything moved in slow motion, and there was no pressure to escalate one's life in fast pace. After Mondo Taitu, we headed to a bar that displayed a sunken ship in the middle with a sign reading 'Swim at your own risk-You Get Cut.' Maybe not the best English, but I got the idea. Taking in the large number of fresh college graduates eager to hit on me, I was not jumping at the chance to hit the dance floor.

The wounds of my past relationship had begun to heal and I had no interest in meeting other men while traveling; I was now backpacking for simple adventure. Tom has taken a liking to me but most of all, I was not in Bocas del Toro looking to start anything with a nineteen-year-old college freshman from Florida. So as Tom eagerly tried to place his hand on my lower back and his tongue on my neck, I pushed him away retreating into my chair, laughing at him trying so hard, then called it a night while the music rocked the night away.

Day 21: June 14, 2008

Bocas del Toro, Panama to David, Panama

After missing the 9:30 AM boat, I waited around for the next one to take me to Changuinola. Sitting on the dock waiting, a little old man brought me a bright purple flower, which I placed in my *Lonely Liar* to remind me of good times on the island. Informing me that the boat had mechanical difficulties, the owner decided to plop me on a second charter back to Almirante. Pushing through the choppy water, it struck me that I had no clue where to go once we pulled into the dock, and I inquired to the man next to me for directions. My plan was to take a bus to David, Panama, located on the western side of the country. Leaving the boat dock, I crossed the road and walked ten minutes to the Almirante bus station, noticing the dirty, loathsome men directly behind me. At the bus station, a boy no older than fourteen informed me that the shuttle to David was actually located on the cross road, two kilometers the other way, outside of town. When I asked for directions, everyone wanted money to show me the way, so I just started walking and hoped I was going the right way. Tires squealed and brakes squeaked to a halt as taxis were eager to drive me out of town. Making it known I planned to walk and refused to pay for the short distance, they blew kisses and sent whistles my way while speeding off. Passing by a group of young children, one shouted *'Gringo'* at me and I found it depressing that although not even five-years-old his vocabulary was limited to such associations. Readjusting my monstrous pack, sweat rolled down my back as I reached the shuttle bus and settled in for the long four-and-a-half-hour trip to David.

Once in David, it was a maze of busses and taxis. I had received an email from another Couchsurfer, Carlos, who said I could stay at his place with his family. Attempting to make a phone call from a Panamanian public phone, I needed a dime, and all I had close by was a quarter. The Panamanian economy works off the American dollar, so my money was good, just in the wrong denomination. Standing in the middle of the bus station, I could not reach my money belt. My two backpacks were wrapped around my body like cellophane, and fear encompassed me as I was worried about being robbed. Sticking out like a sore thumb, I was still dressed in hot-orange running shorts and a black t-shirt, planning for Bocas del Toro weather that morning, not the cool David weather brought in by its mountain location. On one side of me was a group of men peddling knock-off Rolex's, and a few feet away sat a group of women offering fruit. There were no police in sight. Spotting a cellular telephone store, I cradled my way through the door and entered into their public phone booth. Carlos answered on the first ring and said his family would love to have me come to their home. He could not come pick me up, but he did not live too far away. With directions in hand, I headed outside and used my Spanish to bargain with the taxi man to bring me to the house. After arriving, Carlos' family threw their arms around me, grinning from ear to ear and said *"mi casa es su casa"* as they lit up the BBQ and turned up the mariachi music. Carlos had two sisters, one was a professor and the other was studying English. His mom was an attorney. Before I even had time to learn everyone's names, we were having a party and they were teaching me all kinds of Spanish. Panama Spanish was very different from Nicaragua Spanish, so I began learning all kinds of new vocabulary. Carlos' dad was exactly like my dad; he had a bunch of his buddies over that first night. Intent on giving me all kinds of travel advice, they positioned me in the middle of their group and impressed upon me how dangerous Colombia was. Impressed I was going there alone, they wished to know about all of my other travels and then took to asking me all about the *Estados Unidos*. Leading me over to the BBQ, Carlos' dad handed me the utensils, and I was suddenly in charge of cooking the *chorizo*. Skewers of chicken came next and finally grilled fish, all washed down with Milwaukee's Best. Carlos' mom began to tutor me in salsa, and we all danced until midnight, when my eyelids were struggling to remain open. I would definitely need my rest to hang out with this family.

Day 22: June 15, 2008

David, Panama

I awoke in the middle of the night to loud Latin music play-ing outside. Thumping from a car parked on the street, the sound pierced through my window, and I pressed the pillow onto my ears for silence. Knowing that back in the States I could just call the police for a noise complaint, I wondered what would be the correct protocol in David, Panama. Although not sure when I dozed back off to sleep, I awoke at 8:00 AM and was met by the day all independent travelers dream of. Joining Carlos and his two sisters, Lela and Julia, the four of us sang to their Dad for Father's Day before sitting down to a homemade breakfast of *maize pan* biscuits and smoked ham. With my horrid pipes, the earsplitting noise was a gift I knew my father would not want to receive back home. At breakfast Carlos' mom told me to 'go ahead and be selfish, because you are on vacation' and I ate whatever was put before me, dismissing the extra fat that had begun to accumulate on my belly, while piling on more homemade goodness. I decided that I was not training for a marathon or ten-kilometer race anytime soon, so why not enjoy the food?

After lying down flat on the bed and squeezing into my jeans, I added boots to the outfit, and we all piled into the car. Car-los' dad longed to take me to a rodeo that Sunday. Heading into town, we stopped by to visit the other side of the family, who were so excited to meet an American, and I was show-ered in hugs and kisses. The backyard consisted of a large plastic swimming pool where several kids took refuge from the summertime heat wave. Leaving them to their Sunday, we stopped by the ARROCHA store, similar to a Panamanian Wal-Mart, where Carlos' mom got lost in the jewelry section. Pulling Julia and me over, she raised various pieces up to our necks and then insisted on buying both of us new jewelry. An hour later we returned to the car, where Carlos' dad had been sitting, and I told him, "It's just like my family in North Carolina. My dad must wait while mom shops."

Towards the rodeo the countryside of Chiriquí was amazing. Fields were filled with herds of cattle grazing and tumbling, wooden fences, connected by barbed wire; all while surrounded by lush green valleys. We pulled into the rodeo where my family knew everyone, and I was bombarded by all the cowboys and kids who wanted to meet me. Intrigued at my appearance, accent, stories and more, the crowd settled in while I began a round of stories about my travels and life in San Diego. There was a large tent in the distance so Julia and I grabbed a fruit milkshake and made the rounds. Taking shade under a large tree, we watched the twelve cowboys throw back a bottle of tequila as they danced to Mariachi music. When a cowboy saddled his horse later and attempted to lasso, he tumbled off backwards so I hope he learned his lesson about drinking and driving a farm animal. There were little boys in Panama hats practicing their roping techniques on fallen tree branches and cows busting out of the gate every few seconds. The next thing I knew I was up on a horse, and it was riding off somewhere so I turned it around because the inebriated cowboys were shuffling their horses up and down like a stampede, and one of them ran the four legged stallion into a car.

Halfway into the event, Mom, Julia, and I headed over to eat. I was hungry and the smell of roasting meat had been attracting me for some time. There were three red plastic chairs left, and we crammed them together in a corner. There we enjoyed an exemplary chicken soup filled with yucca, broth, and some unidentified veggie I loved, and then follow it with a typical Panama carne jerky. Melting in my mouth, it was so good I went back for seconds. I never found out what it was called. I asked three times but could never get the pronunciation correct. The rain began to come in so we said goodbye to all the rodeo clowns and headed to Playa Barqueta, a dark-sand beach covered in tiki cabanas. Watching the waves come in, it was blatantly clear surfing here was excellent for all my surf buddies back home. The wind blew, and the rain hardened. Taking shelter under a nearby restaurant, we enjoyed *ceviche* and beers before heading back through the powering storm. Julia took over at the wheel, and I joined her in the front seat. Blinded by fog on the windshield, I found myself clearing the glass for Julia every few minutes so she could see the path home. Condensation took over, and heat radiated throughout the car to no assistance. My towel and I were the solution to the problem.

Arriving home I was so happy. It was comforting to be with a family so far away from mine. They had opened their arms and welcomed me into their home without any background or knowledge of me at all. I only hoped that one day I could return the favor to a fellow traveler.

Day 23: June 16, 2008

David, Panama to Boquete, Panama

The next morning I left David at 6:00 AM after tears, hugs, and another incredible breakfast of carne, peppers, biscuits and *queso*. I had long realized that Carlos' family was one of the nicest I was going to encounter on my travels, or ever in life, and was sad to say good-bye. At the bus station, I boarded yet another old rickety vehicle to Boquete, where it turned out I was the only woman on board. I took a seat up front and held on to my ever-expanding bag. The guy to my left tried to strike up a conversation, but the Spanish in Panama was such a different dialect that it was too difficult to understand him. With each passenger that entered the bus I lifted my backpack up and over the guy; he offered to hold on to it, but I did not want to be careless and politely declined. Once we pulled into Boquete, it was a quaint enough town, like a Boone, North Carolina, in Panama. The road I just traveled on was comparable to Hickory from Boone although I had never experienced the first one on a school bus. Digging out my *Lonely Planet,* I walked into the *Hostal Palacios* where I was greeted by Pancho, the over-energetic owner. He sat me down and started to draw me a map of the back country of Boquete which resembled something more of a drunken Christmas tree design. The only thing I could say is he was so proud of his work I could not ask him to produce something more professional. Pancho, I suspected, had never left Boquete, and it was likely had probably hiked every square inch of that town. I did have somewhat of an itinerary for the area so I informed him that I would like to take the 9:00 AM tour of the Cafe Ruiz coffee plantation. With one swift phone call, Pancho smiled and told me I was in.

Leaving the center of Boquete, I walked the two kilometers to the Café Ruiz coffee shop and enjoyed a mocha. No more *café con leche,* my body was calling for steamed milk and whipped cream. Savoring every drop and licking the sides, I was in heaven when the tour guide arrived and drove me south of town to the Café Ruiz plantation. Exiting the vehicle I slowly followed him through the plantation grounds and learned everything I ever wanted to know about coffee. He told me about some coffee that they only grown there in

Boquete, named Geisha. Apparently sixty-kilos cost some-one seventeen-thousand-dollars and are reserved for customers like Donald Trump. There are four steps to this coffee-making process although after all the information piled, I couldn't remember which step was which. My guide reminds me of Melvin from the ATM Caves back in Belize; offering off-the-top facts that I would never use. Next we went to the processing plant, touring the work line where women and men sat for eight hours a day picking out damaged coffee beans for only $8.50/US per day. Watching their work, I attempted to grab spoiled beans and was able to reach for two while the workers picked out over fifty. My guide communicated to us the importance of catching the greatest beans off the conveyer belt as companies paid top dollar for them; spoiled beans would be sold to companies like Folgers and Nescafe for instant coffee. I had been forced to drink Nescafe for weeks in coffee shops mixing it with cups of steamed milk and questioned him on this. He stated that most of the beans found to be inadequate and sold for instant coffee actually stayed within the Central and South American region with the best sent to America and Europe. Communicating his story as we walked past the line, he portrayed his start in the fields as a picker at age ten, then a promotion to line work at fourteen; now he was a tour guide as the result of English studies. Completing the tour, we returned to the main cafe and gained a view of all the packaging. Wearing white doctor coats and cafeteria style net hats, we saw how workers completed sealing bags by hand and then enjoyed more coffee before we were given free Cafe Ruiz grinds and cookies to bring home to the States.

Now that I was jacked up on caffeine, I headed up the road to *Mi Jardin es Su Jardin*. An open garden where visitors were invited to view a wide array of exotic flowers, fish ponds, and windmills, it also contained benches where I sat for hours. As rain began to drizzle, I did not want to lose another *Lonely Planet*, and I noticed a small church in the middle of the landscaped fantasy land where I placed my backpack in the corner behind the vestibule. The only place to catch a dry moment, I opened my peanuts for an afternoon snack, and silently prayed I would not go to hell for eating inside a holy house.

When the rain receded, I checked my watch and realized I was late for a witch hunt. In America we call it hiking, but there was no word in Panama for it. I kept trying to explain hiking to people there, but they did not get it, which was how I ended up walking eight miles around the Boquete countryside that day with my homemade map drawn by Pancho. The trail was not a hike; it was my walking for miles on the side of the road in Boquete. And, while it was beautiful, I was not used to trekking around corners of Central American side lands, dodging vehicles as they careened the thoroughfares. Surrounding me were vast rolling hills with an array of purple and pink flowers, dairy cows grazing up high, and numerous rivers flowing under the bridges I was crossing. Sweat filled my armpits, and I really had no clue where I was. Pancho's map swore I would eventually cross through a place called Palo Alto, pass an Italian restaurant, and begin looping back around to Boquete. I passed an almost invisible fruit stand and asked the little man, *"Donde está es Palo Alto?"* He told me I was there. His fruit stand was Palo Alto. I did not think so. I had not come all that way for papayas and pineapple. So, I kept on walking, taking a little detour because, really, could I be more lost? Then I spotted a cute red barn. When I needed a place to lay my head later, I would return there. Following a path I trailed back to the main 'highway' where I ran into some juvenile school children.

Asking them *"Donde está es Boquete,"* they pointed me down the road while kicking limes toward me. Thanking them, I kicked the lime back. Then they kicked it back. They wanted to play bowling with limes, but I had no clue how much longer Pancho's hike was going to take so I did not have time for this.

Around the corner my brown eyes detected an Italian restaurant, and for the first time I thought Pancho might be on to something. But by now I felt as though I was actually in Italy and hated Pancho so it was not a consolation prize. Suddenly, I spotted a neon sign blinking the words Palo Alto. Looking both ways and crossing over the concrete, I took a left and began up a treacherous hill but not before hearing something to my side. It was a cow lying down sunbathing five feet from me. He eyed me up and down and let out a laggard yawn as if he would not even phase the fact of getting up. Slowly I passed by, hoping not to get attacked by a dairy cow in who-knows-where Panama. After getting to the end of the road, I had only seen new housing developments and turned around to the "main road" to begin back to where I hoped Boquete was. The hillside of Palo Alto was being taken over by retiring Americans; housing developments reminded me of sub-divisions outside of Phoenix. Ecosystems were being destroyed and no one even seemed to care. Beautiful huge homes, complete with swimming pools and three car garages, were being constructed faster than I could walk past them.

Five hours after I began, I finally made it back into town where I realized that Pancho's hostel was really a dump. Should I stay there or cut my seven-dollars and fifty-cents as a loss? So in need of a shower, I strapped my flip flops on and carried my towel into the bathroom. Covered in stray black hairs and missing wall knobs, I tiptoed into the stall and poked my head under the faucet to rinse. Setting my change of clothes down on the side stool, I gasped in fright at the chunks of dust settling in the corner. I would only stay there for one night, and as soon as I dried off, I scurried off to find a new place for the following day. On the opposite side of Boquete I located an appealing, single room at Pension Topas and reserved it right then. Fifty-cents more than Pancho's, the unsoiled, immaculate atmosphere sold me immediately. As I returned to Pancho's, I asked him if it would be okay to leave my bags in the hostel tomorrow, a common practice while travelers enjoy further daily activities. He emphatically told me no, that I would be charged another day. To hell with that, he was not getting anymore of my money. Falling asleep cocooned in my sleeping bag, I constantly woke up with illusions that bed bugs were crawling among my skin.

Day 24: June 17, 2008

Boquete, Panama

It was only 8:00 AM and I was already sweating as I walked the two kilometers towards *Volcan Baru*, the highest point in Panama. I really needed to stop "chasing" volcanoes as I could tell by the two kilometer point that I was going to be sore as hell tomorrow. My body was already suffering and inflamed from the "hike" Pancho sent me on the day before. Joining me to tackle *Volcan Baru* were two Aussies I had met back in Bocas del Toro. The three of us were detached from tourists on the volcano as it lacked any other visitors that sweltering summer morning.

Entrance to *Volcan Baru* was the ranger station where we paid our five-dollar entry fee and began the ten kilometer hike to *La Cina* at the summit which topped out at 3475 m. On a clear day one could see both the Pacific and Caribbean coasts. Beginning our ascent, *Volcan Baru* was all boulders and loose gravel. Establishing a trail to follow was toilsome, and the rugged terrain began to prey upon my knees. The sun pelted down my back and after my trip up *Volcan Maderas*, I had packed twice as much water for this expedition. Since the goal today was over 23 K in total, my pack was heavy, bursting with bananas, power bars and various liquids. Although not as steep as *Volcan Maderas*, *Volcan Baru* provided rugged rocks for climbing in parts, and I was thinking I was definitely getting too old for this. And how the hell was I going to trek around on Machu Picchu for four days in October? My two Aussie friends were more my style though, and we stopped every forty minutes or so to catch our breath as the air was thinner continuing upwards.

There was a time when I would hike anywhere in the world for any length of time. Before I headed out for this trip I told my friends "I am going to hike all the volcanoes and mountains between Nicaragua and Argentina." But as I walked up that volcano in Panama, the only thoughts in my mind were how difficult hiking was becoming. Why the hell was I going forward with the activity that day? There was no enjoyment in it. Basically, the only reason I continued was so I could one day proclaim to my grandchildren that way back when, I had climbed *Volcan Baru*.

Pristine countryside described the views we gained at two kilometers. Boquete dotted with little red houses popped up into view, and soon we passed an ecological garden of some sort on the left. Tiny plants lined up perfectly, protected only by a narrow, wooden fence and some barbed-wire. At seven kilometers the demanding part took over, and we began to march straight up. Not shy about the difficulty, I said "that looks hard" and the Aussies suggested we take a nap. There was not much shade around, and I laid my head onto my backpack, stretching my legs across what gravel I could smooth out. Covering my face with a San Diego Padres baseball cap, the warmth of the sun belted onto my legs. Thirty minutes later, we were ready to go again. As we started uphill I saw a flock of quetzals flying towards me and an impressive overlook on the right; I felt as though I had stepped out of the English countryside with luxurious shades of green and sheep grazing. Almost to ten-kilometers we were met by a green buggy-looking type vehicle that had driven up this volcano...it looked like a jeep on steroids. The driver told us it was not too much further to *La Cina*. Fatigued, we continued on, but once arriving at the top, the clouds had begun to set in and the clear view had diminished. All that work for nothing!

Descending was swift, but I took great caution with my knees. Stumpy rocks left me crawling over them hands first, and when we arrived back to the two kilometer mark, the Aussies remarked, "we should have stopped here; it's the best spot." At the ranger station I asked the ranger to call a taxi for our return. He told me there would be lots of them on the road, but I knew he meant way past where we were dropped off, two kilometers from the entrance. Limping back down the road, I could barely walk anymore; both my legs shook for support, begging me to rest them. We returned to the two kilometer mark the road was desolate. We kept walking. An SUV pulled up full of Americans asking us about the volcano; we tried to talk them out of going. They smiled and told us they would pick us up when they returned. We ended up walking another four kilometer's before I spotted a small car and waved him to slow down. Eyeing me as though I had just robbed a bank, the man and his son said it was probably best if we kept walking because they did not have the room in their car. With their backseat empty I angrily told him the three of us could easily fit in the back, but it would be okay, it was only another four kilometer's into town. Watching them speed off, all of our legs were shaking so bad the three of us could barely hold ourselves up. Ten minutes later we were picked up by some Panamanian construction workers and piled into the back of their truck. They gave us a lift halfway back to town where we started walking around the hills again and finally connected with a taxi. If I had crutches, I would have used them to get back to *Pension Topas* at that point. Once there I slathered Bio-Freeze all over my knees and ankles before falling asleep at 7:30 PM without eating dinner.

Day 25: June 18, 2008

Boquete, Panama to Panama City, Panama

Waking the next morning, I could not get out of bed. My body was so stiff. It was like I had been hit by a truck. After lying there for fifteen minutes, I finally lifted myself up and heard every bone on my body crack. Whatever pounds I had gained from eating ice cream and Central American goodies had been worked off by *Volcan Baru.* I needed coffee.

I went to Cafe Perk across from the main square in Boquete and treated myself to an unbelievable bowl of papayas, bananas, and pineapples probably picked off the tree fresh that morning. I decided to take it easy and preserve my body by spending the day reading in the garden of *Pension Topas* before catching a late bus to David and hopping on the night bus to Panama City. There was a two hour connection in David, and I passed the time by enjoying *empanadas* and viewing Spanish soap operas in the waiting room. There were various busses to take one to Panama City throughout the day, but night busses were more convenient. They cut out the cost of a bus and a hostel, although I had to learn to sleep on a bus and feared my bags may not be with me in the morning.

Night busses are cold throughout Latin America. The night bus from David to Panama City was no exception so I was glad I threw on my jacket at the last minute. At any rate, my nose started running while the air conditioning passed through a vent directed at my head, and I caught a cold somewhere on the ride. Near 3:00 AM I arrived in Panama City. The airport terminal looked nice. My plan was to stay there until the airport opened later in the morning, since it was too late and dangerous to bus it anywhere and too expensive to cab it anywhere alone. Recognizing two backpackers from Bocas del Toro, I connected up to see if they wanted to share a taxi into town. The first taxi driver refused to lead us into the city since we did not want the hostel he recommended. Standing under the fluorescent airport lights, I was groggy and irritated at the corruptness of the system. When a taxi driver finally agreed to drive the three of us to two separate destinations, he did not understand the map I showed him and circled around the Casco Viejo area of Panama City, lost for twenty minutes. Spotting a *policía*, we pulled towards the curb for directions; I reached across the driver and boldly informed the *policía* that we were lost. Shooting me a disapproving look, the cabbie pulled the map from my grasp and finished the conversation. I was in no mood to stay lost at that hour of the morning and thanked the *policía* for his assistance. I was staying three blocks from the President of Panama; it was not hard to find, and when the taxi dropped me off, I noticed we had driven by it more than once. Ringing the doorbell, the night watchman pried open the bars and led me down a dark hallway. Pointing to a bunk bed high up near the ceiling, at 4:00 AM, I crawled into my sleeping bag and slept for four more hours.

Day 26: June 19, 2008

Panama City, Panama

Good Morning, Panama! I was so elated to be in Panama
City which was supposed to be the most cosmopolitan city in
all of Central America. First thing, I ran into a friend from
the Bocas del Toro boat so we headed out into Casco Viejo
together. This area was declared an UNESCO World Her-
itage Site in 2003 so I strolled along the cobbled streets today
to see the restoration process. It reminded me of the East Village of San Diego with dilapidated homes next to brand new
buildings. Walking past the President of Panama's home, I
strolled right through the orange cones and guards, which you
were free to just walk right up to. Nothing like the White
House. Official government policies lacking, there I stood
ten feet from the front door smiling for the camera. Numerous old churches lined Casco Viejo's waterfront although I
had yet to see the 'next Miami' that was written in my travel
guide. Cruise passengers waddled by, easy to spot with their
name badges draped around their necks. A fine target for
robbers, I thought. Leaving Casco Viejo behind, we lugged
our backpacks through the abandoned alleyways seeking out
a bookstore. Detecting none, I quietly assumed no one in
Panama City read. We were told there was a bookstore
uptown and ventured on to the city bus. Covered in flames
and donning the words *El Diablo,* the bus pulled up on a
bustling street corner. We positioned ourselves on the broken
seats and handed the driver twenty-five cents to head across
town. Not entirely sure where to get off, the dark-skinned
Panamanian man behind us asked *"A Donde Va"* and we
offered the bookstores address. At our stop we exited the bus
and prepared to cross a busy freeway during peak rush hour.
Figuring I was going to be hit by a wild driver, I braced for

the worse and took off running without resistance. Turning into the bookstore parking lot, we noticed our friendly man from the bus was following us. Although at a reasonable distance, we did not like the vibe he put out and dodged into the next store we passed. Peeking out the small store windows, he suddenly turned and vanished. Inside the bookstore, prices were equal to the States, and I was forced to purchase another *Lonely Planet* for South America at full price. Set back $34/US, we got back on the bus and returned across town. Stepping through decaying sidewalks and looking down to avoid massive potholes, the two of us dodged more cars to enjoy the best lunch in Panama City at the *Restaurante Mercado del Marisco*, a casual spot above the city's fish market. As we ate, the fisherman paraded below, stringing up their fresh catch. Afterwards we strolled through the aisles and gazed at the variety of shrimp, lobster, and squid. Rosy, pink salmon, larger than me, were displayed across folding tables, eyes bulging at the scales. For two-dollars per pound one could take home shrimp as big as my hands. Fisherman rinsed the floors with spray hoses, and as I walked through, my flip flops slid through the polluted grunge. Leaving the building I smelled as though I had been out on a deep sea expedition for a month.

Later that evening I headed to a Chinese market two blocks from the hostel to scope out some medicine for my head cold. Positioned high up on the shelf was some Vicks 44. Turning it over, I found it to be expired by more than one year. Opting instead for some Panamanian medicine that resembled Alka Seltzer, I purchased two packets and plopped them into a giant orange juice to fend off the cold. My chemistry experiment put me out like a light.

I had a friend coming from San Diego the next day. Her name was Melanie and I was so excited to see her. A little piece of home and a fun travel buddy. I had been working on getting us booked on a boat bound for Colombia later in the weekend. There were only two ways to travel from Panama to Colombia, by boat or plane, and the sailboat trip would be much more fun. Or so everyone had said. But the wait list was up to two weeks and there was only one more spot left on the upcoming ship. So I was keeping my fingers crossed!

Day 27: June 20, 2008

Panama City, Panama

When I woke up this morning, I attempted to join a hostel mate at the Summit Gardens and Sobernia Park, a tropical zoo with exotic animals and birds unique to Panama's jungles. But, we missed the bus by three minutes, and, instead, I decided to make myself another chemistry cocktail of orange juice and cold tablets. Needing more ingredients, I visited the local supermarket. Barely able to breath, as I checked out I began to mix the cocktail. Placing the tablets in the Orange Juice and starting to shake it, the top popped off the Orange Juice, and it looked like a firework in the middle of the store. Apologizing profusely in Spanish, the employee eyed me wickedly and rudely told me to get out of his store. I felt like shit anyway, so I was not really in the mood for an ass kicking, too. Exiting through the metal detectors, I continued repeating in Spanish *lo siento,* but no one seemed to care. Passing out on my bottom bed bunk, three hours later I woke up feeling one-hundred percent better and lazily lounged around the main area of the hostel reading up on my next destination, Colombia. The owner of Luna's Castle hostel introduced himself to me and explained there would be a lavish communal BBQ that evening. Would I like to assist in prepping side items? Cooking has always been a favorite pastime of mine so I jumped on the opportunity to help out and get to know more friends. He put me in charge of potato salad which was a big hit. I told him potato salad was the delicacy I bring to all the BBQ's in San Diego. Grandma Della's potato salad recipe spans the globe and is popular even in Panama! Later that evening, fifty people chowed down on hamburgers, hot dogs and chicken while numerous languages flowed around the table.

As I saved a plate for Melanie she called the hostel to tell me she had already met someone on the plane and was having drinks with them! I remind myself that I had invited my rebellious and crazy friend to Panama and I never knew what she was going to do. Around 10:30 PM she finally strolled in and the first words out of her mouth were "you look like you're getting a gut." Close friends for many years, this was acceptable to hear from her, but hit the nail on the coffin as my chubby thighs had been rubbing together for a week now. I had to stop eating ice cream.

Day 28: June 21, 2008

Panama City, Panama

Many thanks to Melanie for bringing me my new camera to Panama; no thanks to the guy I purchased it from who forgot to send the battery along with it. Now I was in Panama with a new camera and no battery. What now?

I left Melanie asleep at the hostel and headed into the silent streets of Panama City in search of some lithium energy. Walking through the *Cinco de Mayo* section of town, I headed to the PANAFOTO. Armed with nothing but a credit card, passport, and pepper spray, I briskly dodged last night's drunks as they panhandled in the early morning hours. Since this is me we are talking about, the closest PANAFOTO did not have the lithium specialty battery I needed. Sitting behind the counter were numerous cameras similar to mine, but no batteries. How could a store be void of such necessities? Speaking no English, the woman behind the counter explained to me in *muy rapido Espanol* that I should head to *Calle 50.* Possessing no map of Panama, I had absolutely no clue where in the hell I was going or what part of town *Calle 50* was in or where the PANAFOTO would be once I got there. Continuing to ask her for a *mapa,* she drew me two lines and a box on a receipt and said, *"Buenas Suerte."* Walking outside I saw a bus with *Calle 50* written on it and jumped on. Void of any directions, I positioned myself in the front seat of the bus, with a clear view of the city. I had chosen to wear a skirt that day and with each stop men eyed my legs as though I was a twenty-pound turkey on Thanksgiving. Fifteen minutes later I located *Calle 50* and a great big PANAFOTO so I jumped off and headed inside. Holding up my old battery I asked the salesman *"Tu tienes"* and he pointed me towards the back of the store. Unsure of the Spanish word for battery, I simply asked again *"Tu tienes?"* Thank goodness they had it. So I plunked down my credit card and headed back outside. I jumped on the first bus I saw and hoped he was going my way. If not, I would just wing it. For twenty-five cents I could afford to get lost. However, he headed right to *Cinco de Mayo,* but for some reason the bus became stationary for ten minutes, and I started to feel faint and thought I might pass out. Panama was so damn hot. Men and women entered the aisles offering iced drinks and flavored popsicles for rock-bottom prices. There was no circulation through the windows, and I finally got off and walked. It was much cooler although I must hold on to my purse for fear anyone would grab my newly purchased battery.

Once back at the hostel I grabbed Melanie, and we walked back to the bus station for a visit to the Panama Canal. It was another steamy day in Panama, and we oozed with sweat although it was not even 11:00 AM. Of course, we just missed the bus we needed by two minutes, and I was perplexed at how busses in Panama City actually ran on time. Climbing into another one, we decided to take it as far as it would go, then walk to the Canal if we had to. Wiping our brow with Kleenex, the color of the cloth became soiled with scum resting on our face. My pores had swelled, and there were zits breaking out all over my face like I was sixteen again. How women survived year-round in that weather was beyond me. Riding along I asked the driver *"A donde va es el autobus?"* Fortunately, this one goes right by the Canal, too. All those years of taking the bus in San Diego had paid off as now I could get anywhere in any country at any time. Once at the Canal an entry guard asked us *"A Donde Va"* and we let him know we were headed for the causeway. Pointing us down a lengthy sidewalk, we balanced ourselves on a round metal pipe and walked about half a mile to the entry. Handing over our five-dollar entry fee, we were told there were no big ships going through the canal at the moment, just some sailboats. Pushing open the door to the visitor's center, I did not really care; the visitor's center was air conditioned and that suited my current needs to a T. Looking out, the Panama Canal was not that exciting. Just some water and a concrete passageway, but after snapping some photos, I could now say I had been there.

Leaving the Canal, the weather was still roasting outside. I wanted to ask someone if it ever cooled down in his country. Looking to travel from Panama to Cartagena, Colombia, on a sailboat, we still had not secured passageway on a boat by that Friday. Although we were on a stand-by list for a trip at the hostel, Melanie and I decided to head to the yacht club and see if any ships were leaving soon that we could gain passageway on. While we were waiting at the bus station a rainstorm moved into Panama City. The *Lonely Planet* map sent us to the wrong bus station, and after finally connecting to a little shuttle bus, we arrived at the Amador Yacht Club. Full of men eager to provide information, we let them know what we were looking for. The Yacht Club manager shook our hands firmly and informed us no boats were leaving anytime soon. Perhaps we should go down to the Balboa Yacht Club. He said the Balboa Yacht Club was a twenty minute walk back from where we had just come. Though terribly muggy, Melanie and I decided to walk for some exercise. This idea sucked. It was one-hundred degrees outside and not twenty minutes by foot. Perhaps only by car. My blood sugar was lowering and with each crack in the sidewalk I felt more faint. Spotting a dollar store of sorts, we pulled inside. A bored-looking woman sat behind the counter, and I asked if she sold any crackers. No, only cookies and sodas. I scanned the shelves and decided on some generic white Oreos to see me through the afternoon; simply not healthy, but enough to keep me going. An hour later we had still not arrived at the yacht club and sulked on the sidewalk as we debated to head back to the hostel without booking a boat to Colombia. A man pulled up in a car gabbing on his cell phone, and we knocked on the windows inquiring in which direction was the yacht club. He said he would take us there; it was just up the road. Looking at each other, we figured together we could overpower him if we had to, but kindness prevailed and he dropped us off a few moments later. We arrived dripping wet at the yacht club, which was really just a bar with some boats docked out front. I would have been afraid to get on any of those boats as they might break down as soon as they set sail. Patronizing the bar were retired men, scalps covered with pepper-gray hair, if they were not already balding. Watching them down cheap beer, I found myself wondering if I was on the coast of Galveston, not Panama City. Swigging down two glasses of water, we got the hell out of there. Across the street we noticed a free shuttle that was taking people to and from Casco Viejo for a big music festival. The men were more than eager to provide a ride back to Casco Viejo, and I was happy we had finally found some luck in our day.

After returning to Casco Viejo, we searched the market for some much needed items, such as pineapples, mangos, rum, and ice to make daiquiris. Scouring the supermarket for ice, we had a problem. There were no ice freezers located at the front of the store, as in the USA, so we asked in the liquor section. They sent us back to the front of the store, and the workers there sent us upstairs. Why would ice be located upstairs, we thought? In the far corner of the second floor we located ice chests. No. No. No. *Hielo* is the word for ice in Spanish, and after three laps around the supermarket, we were getting nowhere. Back out on the street, we dipped into a wanna-be mini market and asked the ten-year old girl behind the counter for *hielo*. One bag was seventy-five cents. We took two; no more worries. Across from her was a little old man selling mangos. Attempting to bargain with him was harder than finding my hidden Christmas presents, and he refused to throw in four mangos for the price of three. See-ing as he was so stingy, I left to buy from another vendor; turned out the little man held a monopoly on Panama City mangos. I had learned bargaining was a way of life in Cen-tral America and refused to go back to his stall. Melanie walked back over, and in the end he threw in the fourth fruit. Toting our heavy bags back to the hostel we fired up the blender and passed the frigid, fruity drinks around. Happi-ness flooded the hostel before a large group of us headed to the music festival.

Preparing to leave, Melanie and I were already feeling a strong buzz. Knowing that Panama City was a dangerous city, I warned her to be on guard all evening. While picking out a dress to wear I re-iterated the dangers that come with being a white, blonde American woman in Latin America. Know where you are and who you are with at all times. There is no need to flaunt what you have because the men here are already attracted to you as a blonde American. Leaving the hostel, we walked two blocks down with a large group of hostel mates and began to enjoy listening to the typical Panama music, and I think the Panamanians enjoyed watching our group dance like crazy! Apparently there were actual moves to the music, but we did not really know them so it was booty-dancing for all. Jumping up on stage Melanie and I joined in with the band for guitar playing and dancing before I met two Panamanian women and ended up talking with them for an hour in Spanish; it was always a good time to practice. As midnight came calling I decided it was time to leave. The festival was a lot of fun, but the late hour called for dangers, and I was already too drunk to be out in Casco Viejo so late. Waving goodbye to everyone, I found a *turismo policía* to walk me the two blocks back to Luna's Castle where I crashed for the evening. At 6:00 AM I awoke to Melanie's empty bed. Figuring she had met someone and was still out having a good time, I turned over and went back to sleep. Thirty minutes later I felt a finger poking me awake. Twisting to my right I was met by Melanie, wearing nothing but a faded blue hospital gown drenched in blood. Her left arm was wrapped in bandages; her hair tussled like a rag doll that had been thrown in the corner. Sitting up I was perplexed at her state when she whispered, "I was mugged," as tears filled her eyes. Accompanying her was a tall Panamanian man with broad shoulders and dark hair. Speaking perfect English, he handed me two prescriptions and told me she needed medicine and they needed to be filled immediately. Dazed and confused, I propped myself up listening as Melanie filled me in on the night before. She had met the guy sitting next to her now, and they had left the music festival. He had taken her to a bar nearby, where they proceeded to take body shots off each other over the next few hours. Leaving the bar at a dangerous hour near 3:00 AM, they were surrounded by a group of five people requesting Melanie's purse. When she attempted to fight back, they held a gun to her head and slit her arm with a broken beer bottle. Within minutes the *turismo policía* had placed her in the back of their car and carried her off to the hospital, where she was stitched up.

Helping her into bed, I lay back down myself to catch a few more hours of sleep. The room was muggy and humid, mixed with a hangover left me popping migraine pills until mid-day. By the time I woke back up, Melanie had passed out in the middle of the floor, and I knew there was no way we could travel into Colombia that evening. I worked to re-book our flight and after waking up the *turismo policía* came calling in the afternoon, advising us they had two people in custody and needed Melanie to accompany them to the station for a line-up. Unlike line-ups in the United States, Melanie would see her attacker face to face and declined the line-up. She also refused to give a statement. Heading to the pharmacy the next day, Melanie and I attempted to obtain antibiotics for her wounds. As we paid, the man behind the counter asked her if she was the girl from the newspaper. Confused, we shook our heads; then he pulled out the newspaper. Melanie was on the front page being carried into the hospital. And while she distinctly requested no attention back at the hostel, that night while changing her wounds, there were no shortage of bystanders.

Day 30: June 23, 2008

Panama City, Panama to Cartagena, Colombia

AIRES Airlines. Since we had never secured a sailboat trip to
Cartagena, we booked our flight to Colombia on the little, no
name airline after some English boys at Luna's Castle told us
about the discount transportation. A new friend of Melanie's,
named Carlos, called and offered us dinner and a ride to the
airport. He was late, and after he showed up there was rush
hour traffic in Panama City, so much that his BMW over-
heated-he tried to explain that in "this city" that happens a lot.
I tried to explain to Melanie later that Carlos was a dumbass.
After the overheating problem, we switched cars with his
friend who then needed gas and after three toll booths, we
finally arrived at the airport. Over one hour later. But not
before Carlos and his friend lit up a joint to share with each
other in the backseat. Exactly what I wanted; to smell like
marijuana as I checked in for a flight to Colombia. Attention,
Carlos, I was not looking to spend twenty years in a Central
American prison.

At AIRES they made us check our backpacks because apparently we would be boarding the smallest airplane ever. As I
stepped through immigration, I realized that my boarding
pass had Melanie's name on it, but the immigration officer
did not seem to care as I glided on through. Security in Central America never seemed to amaze me. Melanie and I
searched though the airport to obtain food, but there was no
place to eat, only duty free shops. Panama City had a long
way to go before it impressed me as the "next Miami." As we
waited for AIRES to board, we took the opportunity to walk
through the airport several times and get some exercise.
When we loaded onto the plane, there were only six people

joining us for the journey. We laughed because back at the hostel, the English guys described the plane as held together by duct tape so I was thinking this was a "wing and a prayer."

A few minutes later all I heard was rattling, and I was like "please get me to Colombia." It was only an hour flight to Cartagena, but they served us a whole dinner and some directions to a *supermercado* for when we landed. Seriously, American airlines need to take note. Upon touch down, we walked onto an airstrip where no one else was and walked directly through security. They were basically holding up a sign saying 'Welcome to Colombia!' Our bags were waiting for us, nice and neat next to baggage claim, and so far Colombia was making a good impression upon me. Sharing a cab with another passenger, the three of us hopped into the taxi and attempted to pull over at a roadside place for food. I stayed in the vehicle and locked all the doors; watching as Melanie and the other passenger were surrounded. There were too many guys interested in us, and I screamed, "Back in the cab!" My life was not worth tacos and beer, and I was not interested to find out what this gang of Colombians had planned. I instructed the taxi driver to take us to *Casa Viena* in the Getesmani District. Well after midnight, the streets were deserted but for bums and drug dealers. Litter surrounded us, and a putrid smell filled the air; I was not sure if it was piss or water. All I knew was I needed to get inside fast. Buzzing *Casa Viena*, the woman explained to me they were full. We could walk down the street to *Hotel La Casona.* As we reached into our pockets to pay the cab driver, a beggar appeared and would not go away. I was not about to pull out my money while he was there. Stepping closer to my bag, I figured it was a good time to scream like hell and hit him with a baseball bat. If I had one. Our male counterpart pulled out a wad of cash, and I wished I could hit him instead. Setting us up to be robbed, I left him with the beggar and cab driver and began walking down to *Hotel La Casona*. Armed with my pepper spray against the beggar, I did not really expect it to do much against the guns and machinery they had there in Colombia. Once at the hotel, Melanie and I settled in a double room and then argued with the hotel owner over the exchange rate for twenty minutes. Knowing damn well what it was, I fought for a while until I became tired and agitated, then cut my losses and went to sleep. This was the second person in Colombia who plainly just did not want US dollars or who worked in tourism but had no clue what the exchange rate was. Fucking recession.

Day 31: June 24, 2008
Cartagena, Colombia to Playa Blanca, Colombia

With five hours of sleep under our belts we awoke at 6:00 AM and left Cartagena aimed for Playa Blanca. The lady at *Hotel La Casona* directed us to go the *Centro de Convenciones* to catch a *lancha* called Alcatraz, but her story seemed a little skewed. We decided to follow the *Lonely Liar* which is how we ended up waiting at the *Mercado Bazurto* for over an hour seeking out a bus to the beach that never came while Colombian men whistled at us all morning. It gets really old having men drive by and hiss at you or call you 'baby.' Traveling through so many Latin American countries, I had yet to realize if they truly believed women found those tactics sexy. Surely, no woman fell for it or said "Oh, thank you for whistling at me. Now I will hop in your ratty old bus and bring you back to America with me."

One hour later, with no Playa Blanca bus in sight, a stumpy little man and his dirty, sweaty friend struck a deal with us to 'drive us to the beach' which in reality was to drive us to the other side of the market to the boat dock where his friend was waiting to haul tourists to Playa Blanca. After I bargained with the Captain, he promised we would leave in twenty minutes for $4/US per person. We ended up sitting in the boat for an hour while more tourists showed up. Meanwhile, the original stumpy man leaned over our seats and begged us for money because he so generously helped us find the way to Playa Blanca. Shouting to him that he did not deserve any money, I added that he was a thief. The first lesson in begging is to refuse the beggar, or less more beggars will appear. When he would not disappear, Melanie attempted to give him a US dollar, and he handed it back to her telling her he only accepted pesos. Laughing profusely, I shouted in Spanish to him that 'beggars could not be choosers.' By now it was past 8:00 AM, and we were hungry. Walking into the main marketplace, we attempted to order breakfast. Handing the woman a five-dollar bill, she refused to cook us rice and eggs, shaking her head and saying no to the US dollar. Glancing to her left, she inquired with her son about the exchange rate. I was happy to assist in the economy department, but she shooed me out of her kitchen. I could not figure out if it was because twenty-five percent of all counterfeit United States money was coming from Colombia or because they truly did not know the exchange rate; either way it was impossible to give away the US dollar there. In every other Latin American country, except Colombia, they had begged for the US currency. We had arrived in Colombia at midnight and had been nowhere near a bank so the opportunity to get pesos has been non-existent. There was no way to exchange money anywhere. I was at a loss for how difficult spending my cash was.

Returning to the boat, we sat there with our stomachs growling. Sharing a granola bar, I took in our surroundings.

Poverty-stricken Colombia was upon us. The high-rises of Cartagena were in the far-off distance. To my right were hard-working men, carrying machetes to cut boat rope and dice up fish. Each worker passed off bags of rice and bundles of bananas to each other, loading up provisions to be dropped at neighboring islands. Empty plastic bottles and candy wrappers littered the water's edge, and dogs wandered by aimlessly searching for scraps. Once the boat captain came to collect our money for the trip, the price suddenly shot up from four-dollars per person total to thirteen-dollars each. He was crazy. I had been taking *lancha's* all over Central America, and they did not cost $13/US per person. All the other *Gringos* were whispering to me "That is the price we paid," and instead of telling them they overpaid to their face, I decided my life was not worth $26/US bucks and threw down the money. Giving me a blank look, the guy had the audacity to tell me he needed us to pay him extra money because it was going to cost him extra money to change the money from US dollars to pesos. We were fed up.

Melanie shouted "Yeah, we understand, but that is not our problem." Handing me all the money back, he began to physically remove our two backpacks out of the boat. He would rather not have any money at all than do business with us. As I was trying to compromise with him, he started talking to the male next to me because he was a man, and I was a woman! As if that did not piss me off enough, he acted as if I was not even there, simply translating through the other passenger. Finally, another backpacker handed me some pesos, and I offered him my US dollars. The backpacker exclaimed, "What a great deal for me!" I know. That is what I did not understand. Journeying through the sea we began to hear from other backpackers that this was happening all throughout Colombia. No one would accept the US currency there, and they had encountered people not understanding the exchange rate as well.

The ride to Playa Blanca was full of jolts. Several times I believed we would flip over as part of a circus stunt. The Captain was a horrible driver. Coming in to Playa Blanca, there was no dock. We simply anchored ten feet from shore and jumped off into the water where we walked five steps to a shack called "Mama Ruth's." Nothing more than a few tiki huts and hammocks, Melanie and I scored a double bed for a total of five-dollars per night. Tossing our bags in the sand, we threw on our bikinis and ran into the Caribbean Sea. It was so warm, both the water and the sun. The difference between Playa Blanca and Panama City was that I could cool down in the serenity of an open ocean. Spending the rest of the day dozing in and out, while reading my latest novel and swimming, Playa Blanca was like being a character on 'Lost.' For lunch Mama Ruth served up an enormous plate of fresh fish, veggies, *papas fritas* and fried plantains. That night I watched the sun go down while perched in a chair with my feet dipped in the water. Just like a Kenny Chesney song. Not a bad way to visit Colombia after a crazy start.

Day 32: June 25, 2008

Playa Blanca, Colombia

I was staying on Cast Away Island. All I needed was a volleyball named Wilson and I could have been Tom Hanks. Mama Ruth cooked meals with fire and wood, people slept in hammocks and makeshift tents, and we ate only fish and rice. I loved it because there were no phones, emails, or TV's-it was a nice place to get lost for a while. It was steaming though. When I wasn't taking refuge in the water, the sun pelted down on me like a mid-western hail storm taking out a new car.

Day 33: June 26, 2008

After awhile I truly did start to feel like Tom Hanks on that beach. No showers, no people, the bathroom consisted of gravity pulling a bucket of water down to wash away my business. Too afraid to enter the *baño* at night, I walked a few feet onto the beach before squatting next to a bush and scurrying back to my bed. I was always worried a dog, donkey, or some new breed of snake would sneak up and grab me. During the days I cooled off by swimming in the clear Caribbean Sea. Even though it was not much colder, the momentous refreshment it brought was an absolute must. Slathering on SPF 30 constantly, my body winced at the damage that could come at constantly being under the earth's radar there. Water tasted foul on the beach with a hint of fish smell to it. Thank goodness I had Crystal Light packets to wash away the taste. I had brought my Nalgene bottle to help the environment, but even the purified water needed help.

Secluded on Playa Blanca with nothing but US dollars, I paid Mama Ruth with my money. Her son told me that US money was worthless to Colombians, but I explained to Mama Ruth that I had no *pesos* and no *mas dinero*. Since his English was reasonably good I considered the conversation over and got on a boat back to Cartagena. Melanie had decided that she wanted to stay and enjoy the beach a while longer. I wanted to see other parts of Colombia because I never knew when I would be back to the country. Before we separated she said she thought I was brave for doing what I was doing-traveling the world alone. I didn't consider myself brave. I just thought I was doing what anyone would if they had been in my situation. With free time from a career, no relationship commitment, and no kids to look after. It only then began to occur to me that I might be brave. All along I knew I had been traveling to dangerous places, but to me it was just another adventure in my life.

Leaving Playa Blanca I was granted some free porn. At the edge of the beach, two people were partaking in free loving on the beach and I scurried past them as his hands removed her bikini bottoms. As we pulled out of Cartagena, we searched the beach twenty minutes looking for two people who had really "missed the boat". Finding them, they were the couple I saw earlier having a great time with each other on the beach. They joined us on the already packed boat as though we were illegal's from Cuba bound for Miami. Everyone possessed a life vest but me and two other *Gringos;* we were fully aware they had shoved us on board to try to make a quick extra twenty-dollars. When we arrived in Cartagena, I went straight to the bank and grabbed some pesos so I could obtain some fruits and veggies at the marketplace; then I rounded the corner to Hotel Holiday where I took a MUCH NEEDED shower. I had gone days without a shower before, in Joshua Tree and Death Valley. But now I really stunk. Three days on an island in Colombia, I looked like I was a baby just rescued from a well. After cleaning up I walked to the market and bought ten mangos, three bananas, a meat/potato kabob, and sausages, all for fewer than three-dollars. The smoke from the sausages stretched through the air and I could not wait until they met my mouth. Leaving the food stall, I tripped walking down the street trying to eat the food so fast.

Back at the hostel two friends from Playa Blanca stopped by. We all made plans for tomorrow night before I crawled into bed.

Day 34: June 27, 2008

Cartagena, Colombia

I fell in love with Cartagena right away. The first morning I
woke up early and set out on a walking tour of the city.
Beginning at the Parque de Centro, I then led myself into the
Puerta del Reloj, the main gateway of the inner town. Behind
the large clock sat the Plaza de los Coches, a square that was
once used as a slave market. The old town was filled with
colonial arches and *balcones*. Winding streets and floral
overhangs reminded me a lot of Antigua, but I found Cartagena superbly more beautiful. Nearby was Plaza de Bolivar,
which displayed Inquisitor's instruments of torture, pre-
Colombian pottery, and works of art from the colonial and
independence periods. There were hundreds of street vendors
there trying to sell me everything from a new cell phone to a
Panama hat. If I heard a man call me *chica* one more time, I
was going to lose it. It was impossible to enjoy a walk without fearing a man may grab me, toss a bag over my head, and
drag me into a dark building. Constantly on my guard, I
turned in every direction each time I pulled my camera out of
my case before snapping a photo and pushing it back into my
pocket.

Around the corner was the Museo del Oro filled with a collection of gold and pottery from the Sinu culture and a *catedral* that was in view from a small, but pretty, park, filled to
the brim with old Colombian men watching the day go by.
Legs crossed and benches packed, men gathered to play
checkers and smoke cigars while they people watched the
city. So I sat with them and joined in for a while. Down the
street was the Iglesia de Santo Domingo which was the city's
oldest church and the most beautiful church I had ever been
in to that point. I joined in for the end of mass and even

though I was not Catholic, the service was very touching. Catholics of all ages, races, and sizes bowed on their knees, praying before the high crosses. Tears streaked down their cheeks, and I watched as a young woman took confession in a corner. Priests meandered in the aisles, blessing each attendee on their foreheads, while tourists brushed their sides and looked up with video cameras.

The beginning of one of many walls to protect Cartagena from pirates also began near the church so I headed outside and stepped up on top. The wall was surrounded by monuments and art dedicated to many men with roles in Cartagena's past. It reminded me of San Diego's waterfront, paying tribute to those who have given to others. Scrambling along the cobblestone, I enjoyed exploring the wall and playing in the tunnels and cannons that were built to protect Cartagena from pirates. Finally, I simply got lost in the streets and wandered while taking in the elegant beauty.

Later in the afternoon, I joined up with a Czech friend from my hostel, and we walked around the city at dusk. First, we headed to the Castillo de San Felipe de Barajas, begun in 1639 but not completed until one-hundred-and-fifty years later. A grand stone fortress built to keep pirates out, it was topped off with a flag. As the sun faded behind the majestic churches, we sat in front of the impressive Iglesia de Santo Domingo and enjoyed listening to the bells ring and experienced a mime play with children as nighttime activity began in Cartagena. There was music playing throughout the city, and it was so alive! We then headed back to the Hotel Holiday and put on proper clothes before setting out to find a restaurant called El Bistro and meet up with my new hostel friends. Speaking in Spanish, but accenting with my Southern tongue, several people steered me to La Visteria. After several laps around the low-lit alley ways of Cartagena, the two of us settled near the Museo Naval del Caribe, where Cartagena's feel was that of like the San Diego Gaslamp. Horse-drawn carriages filled the streets, musicians lit up the night, gaslamps provided sight, chic twenty-something's walked around everywhere, and a cool breeze could be felt off the waterfront. Taking our seats, we ordered two Cuban cigars. Not being a smoker, I watched as mine continuously went out and needed to be re-lit. I kept asking, "Is it lit," while my friend just laughed. Even though we were already smoking, panhandlers surrounded us, opening their tattered jackets revealing long, skinny café cigars, offering us a good price. Jovially we held up our cigars and shook them away. As we moved towards home, we stopped back by the Puerta del Reloj where colorful dressed teenagers filled the square dancing. The girls resembled Chiquita the Banana Lady, and the boys wore nothing but white cotton pants. Performing barefoot, the group moved throughout the crowd, waving their hips from side to side and lifting each other high into the sky. Clanking two more beers together, we ended the night watching Cartagena close down.

Day 35: June 28, 2008

Cartagena, Colombia

It was the end of June and Cartagena was hot. It was so hot that I walked one-hundred meters and I had already sweated through my tank top and there was no reason to put on deodorant. I smelt like you had been working on the farm without a tractor, picking cotton by hand in the middle of a Texas heat wave. It took the fun out of vacation. I wondered how people lived there all the time.

On that day, I joined Lynda from Argentina to walk towards the New Town of Cartagena called Bocagrande. It was a 2 K distance, but in the Cartagena heat and humidity it felt like 10 K. Along the way we waded in the water provided by the Caribbean Sea. Mid-summer tourists cluttered rows of white beach chairs, searching for shade beneath *Imperial* beer sponsored tents. Perched on a rock was a Colombian body builder who looked out of place in the line of pot-bellied old men donning Speedo's. The sand felt like hot coals beneath my feet, and I rushed from the water breaks to keep them cool. Arriving in the streets of Bocagrande, they were nothing to be too impressed with. Mainly the downtown of the city, with high-rises and condos, it included a nice Hilton Hotel which I made sure to inspect for an industry friend back in the states by going inside to see if the HVAC worked. It did and felt quite nice after my long walk.

Returning back to the hostel, I crashed onto my bed wearing nothing but my bra and panties. I did not care who saw me; the humidity was too much to bear. Lying there I cooled off by devouring three mangos and allowing the juice to run down my chest. The problem with devouring mangos so rapidly was that I found tiny, little strings remaining in my teeth and gums. Utilizing my tweezers and travel mirror, I attempted a surgical procedure in my mouth and gently pulled out the strings one by one until I could finally run my tongue over my teeth again.

Later that evening I sat in the courtyard waiting for Melanie to return from Playa Blanca when in walked a male traveler from New Zealand asking me "Are you Jen?"

"Yes" I replied. Then he proceeded to tell me that he and Melanie had taken beds at another hostel down the street. I was upset since I had brokered a deal with my hostel to save her their only room left that evening. Instead she only seemed to care about herself and did not even have the courtesy to walk down the street to greet me in person. Instead she sent her newest 'boy toy.' An hour later I still had not seen her so I went around the corner where I found her talking on the phone with a travel agent making arrangements to head back to America. Was she planning on telling me? We were supposed to head into Ecuador tomorrow for a week of school. She nodded in my direction then went back to her conversation; I headed back to my hostel. As I joined some friends to head out for the last night in Cartagena in walked Melanie. She told me she planned on leaving and wanted the money I owed her ASAP (when we booked the tickets to Colombia she insisted on putting them both on her credit card and then I would pay for her portion of the Ecuador school program). I was tired of her sour attitude and told her I would get it to her in the morning, but all I had was Colombian pesos. Is that what she wanted? Would she rather not wait until I was back in the States and could give her American currency that was more valuable?

"Whatever just get it to me" she said. I explained to her that there was no way I was headed to a Colombian ATM after dark, but I would leave it for her in the morning at the hostel. "Fine, see you later then" she said and walked off.

I was done and over it. I did not come to Latin America to hook up with random guys and seek out free drinks that could possibly be drugged. Traveling as a single American woman was dangerous. She should know that by now and I was over her little tactics. We were supposed to travel together and have a good time, but all she wanted to do was meet men and hook-up. I had better things to do, like see the sights of the country, and not end up as a CNN special.

When I was finished getting ready, a large group from the hostel emptied itself onto the streets of Colombia where everyone at the Hotel Holiday joined up at the Puerta del Reloj. Clambering for yellow chairs, we attempted to move our tables together and join forces, but were dissuaded by the Colombian waiters. Instead, fifteen of us were forced to sit around a table for two. When the rain came, we stayed and watched as all the local tourists ran for cover. Water never hurt anyone, and this was no exception. As the storm grew, our group grew antsy, and we carried our chairs against the wall of the bar. Swaying with the music I let the night carry me away and pretended I was in Cuba. Cartagena was how I imagined Cuba to be, full of nightlife, cigars, and strong rum flowing between friends. There were no worries.

We waited for the rain to subside, and when it failed to, we splashed through it towards the Havana Club. Slipping on my flip flops, I braced myself on every statue in town until arriving at the front door. Entering, I could hear music filling the air. Sounds from trumpets, bongos, and guitars led me to the dance floor, where I began to move in circles without a partner. Accepting mesmerizing looks from the crowd, I continued flowing to the rhythm. It was my last night in Colombia, and in two days I would have to start studying Spanish again. After this, there would be no more freedom, so I jumped up onstage and joined up with the band. When I curled up with my pillow, I was passionately dreaming of salsa inspired attractions.

Day 36: June 29, 2008

Cartagena, Colombia to Quito, Ecuador

Okay, so let me just preface and say that my adventure from Cartagena to Quito was experienced on five hours of sleep.

What sounded great the night before felt like shit the next morning as I woke up at 7:00 AM and wondered what could cure my Havana Club hangover. First things first, after my alarm went off, I grabbed a much needed cup of java at the Gato Negro coffee shop before heading to the airport. Hailing down a cab, I hopped in the backseat, where the driver was all too eager to keep adjusting his mirror for a better view of my chest. Alerting him in Spanish to focus his eyes on the road, I wanted nothing more than to close my eyes and catnap it on the way, but now I was terrified he was going to drive me into a dark garage somewhere.

Pulling up to the curb at the airport, I checked in at AVIANCA. The petite woman behind the counter wore square eyeglass and looked me up and down. I knew I probably reeked of cigars and rum, but no matter, I just wanted to exit Colombia. As I handed her my passport, she asked me, *"A donde va despues Quito?"* I responded, "Peru." It was not a total lie. I was planning to go to Peru, just not by air. My plan was to bus it everywhere; it was cheaper. The borders in Colombia simply were not safe for me to cross by bus and virtually impossible from Panama to Colombia, due to the Darien Gap. Officially, I was supposed to have a return ticket out of Ecuador, but border authorities rarely asked for proof of this and hardly ever bothered backpackers. They knew we were going from one place to the next. The attendant asked for my proof of exit out of Ecuador into Peru. Since she was not a border official, I looked her straight in the eye and lied, telling her I had a plane ticket out of Ecuador, but it was in my email. Not content with this answer, she asked for my proof back to the United States. Head pounding and limbs tired, I wanted nothing more than to strangle her at that moment. I had my ticket out of Colombia; why couldn't she let me go? I told her the return ticket to the States was also in my email. That was a lie as I had not bothered purchasing one yet since I was planning to return to the States in December and had months to plan my return home. Holding my passport, she proceeded to tell me how I must hold proof of a return ticket or I would not be allowed to board. Moving forward with her story she started on about the political history of Ecuador and Colombia, and God knows that my hangover was in no mood for that. Interrupting her history lesson, I told her I would deal with the Ecuador border official if he asked for my proof of return to Colombia although in all honesty, why would he? I was not a Colombian citizen, and I had a fifty-pound backpack attached to me. Standing there, I sure as hell was not about to buy a last-minute ticket on AVIANCA. After hassling back and forth, finally, she printed up a 'fake' boarding pass for me, and I left my *mochilla* with her, hoping to see it in Quito.

After landing in Bogota, I took a shuttle bus from one terminal to another. More exercise with less energy. The main terminal was a maze of stairs and gates, and I must have looked frazzled because a security guard spotted me like *Where's Waldo* and asked, *"A Donde Va?"* Showing him my boarding pass for Quito, he told me to follow him to the international terminal and directed me up some stairs. More exercise. I really needed some damn coffee. Arriving at the top of the stairs, I immediately spotted a McDonald's and knew if all else failed, they would have McCafe coffee there, but there were lots of restaurants, exactly the remedy I needed. Noticing a *Crepes and Waffles,* I decide on that, since some friends in Cartagena had recommended it a few days ago. Taking a seat in a corner booth, my body collapsed in the cushion. When the server walked over, I began to salivate at the sight of the menu and immediately ordered a spinach and *queso* crepe, accompanied with a *café con leche*. I savored every bite, but decided it was not enough and went ahead and ordered a chocolate crepe, and another coffee for dessert. Feeling the chocolate and ice cream mix together and melt was like tasting an explosion in my mouth.

I was in heaven and never wanted to leave the confines of *Crepes and Waffles*. Unfortunately, I had to. Stepping across the terminal, I attempted to go to gate one. Handing the guard my boarding pass, she shook her head disapprovingly and pointed me down a long corridor. Apparently I was in the domestic flight area, and there was another gate one in the same terminal. After handing my bag to the security screener and running it through the x-ray machine, I was told that my Coleman camping wrench was a forbidden object. I found this interesting since the object had made it through numer-ous airport screenings so far. Forced to turn around and leave, I returned to the AVIANCA desk agents and explained that even though I had no luggage, I must somehow get this wrench to Ecuador. Three women and one man offered me assistance in Spanish telling me there was no way to get the wrench to Ecuador, and I was beyond reasoning with AVIANCA that morning. Finally, the male agent behind the counter located a tiny box (think cell phone size) and covered it with AVIANCA packaging tape. Not really expecting the wrench to arrive in Quito, I returned back to security where I handed my bag to the security screener once more and watched as my pepper spray made it though. It was always the little things in life that never ceased to amaze me. It was a good thing though because I would have gone down kicking and screaming over the pepper spray. It was the only item getting me through Latin America.

Fifty yards in, I handed my passport to the immigration offi-cial who eyed me up and down twice before saying I did not resemble my picture. He questioned me on my address, birth date, and social security number and did not want to let me pass through. Okay! I know I had been traveling a while and been wearing my hair in a ponytail for several months, but seriously, he should know to NEVER tell a woman she does not look nice! Then, I passed my bag to the Colombian military for a drug check, but the officer barely looked up to ask me what goods I had inside. I assumed it was reassuring to know I did not look like a drug smuggler. There were dogs, too, but they were busy with someone else and about ten Colombian military men with guns so big I dared not breathe for fear the gun's safety let loose on me. Next came the pat down, which involved spreading my legs and a feel up from the Colombian officials before I continued on to my gate. Not trafficking drugs myself, after that little episode, I was not sure how anyone actually did it.

On the plane ride to Quito the turbulence proved to be tremendous, and I wanted nothing more than to hold the hand of the guy next to me. Not wanting him to freak out like a manic-depressant, I chose not to suddenly grab him for support and instead threw on my I-Pod and listened as Norah Jones soothed me to sleep.

Sailing over Quito the mountains were beyond beautiful. I could tell from the miniscule window view that I was going to enjoy my time in Ecuador. Bouncing on the runway, one tire at a time, I was grateful to touch down. At immigration I took my place in the long line of people returning to their homeland. Their passports were worn with travel, and I could barely make out the word Ecuador stamped on the front of many of them. Moving to the front the numbers lit up each time a person stepped forward. An immigration official announced it was my turn, and the woman greeted me in an overly upbeat tone as I approached. She said nothing more than, "Enjoy Ecuador" as she stamped my passport. So much for needing a forwarding ticket. I wanted to send an email back to that agent at AVIANCA. Waiting for my luggage to come, I stood and watched as the little, tattered box rolled on by, bringing with it my Coleman wrench. Where was my backpack? Fears entered my mind, and I knew I would be lost in Ecuador with no clothes or supplies. The luggage wheel continued to move in a circle, and there was no sign of my bag until finally the last piece of luggage dropped down the chute and I spotted the bright blue sack dragging along. Relieved, I squatted down and positioned it into place before exiting into the lobby where I was greeted by a man who shouted, "Are you Jenifer?" "Yes" I replied. He informed me that he was there to take me to my new family's house. That was a good thing since I had no clue where I was going when I walked off that plane. Prior to arriving in Ecuador the volunteer program had sent an email stating I would be living with a family, but nothing further. I was not sure if I would need a hostel that evening; it was already late, and I was too tired to read a map of Quito. The man asked me to wait on the side of the airport terminal. This turned into forty-five minutes until he came back and said it would be 'a while' for my driver. Handing me a pink voucher for the taxi, he scribbled the address of the family and ushered me outside. Standing on the sidewalk, I looked dazed and confused in a wash of Ecuadorians. A small woman asked me, *"A Donde Va,"* and I showed her the address. Since I did not know where I was going, it was more like a scavenger hunt. She placed me inside a taxi, and off I went. Opening up my map of Quito, I scrounged for the location, but the address was nowhere to be found on my map so I had NO CLUE where I was going. Leading me was the oldest taxi driver in Ecuador. He said he knew the area well; yet somehow twenty minutes later we were on our way up a hill, and he began asking me, "Where is your family's house?" How in the hell did I know? I had only been in Quito for an hour! The next ten minutes was filled with the two of us driving back and forth on a street that forgot to include street signs during its conception. Numbers were obsolete, and the light inside the cab was so dim I could barely make out the address. Finally, I spotted a woman standing outside waving us down. She laughed as I stumbled out of the taxi, dragging my two packs. Looking up I realized the house was nice. It was the nicest house I had been in since leaving San Diego. And I was not presentable or nice. I smelled like sweat and urine and airports and looked even worse. My hair had not been washed in a few days; it was pulled back in a ponytail, the dirt on my face was thick…and upon entering the home I was in awe. There were guards out front, controlling who entered and left the building and it was necessary to enter through two gates. Once upstairs, there was fine china and I had a satellite TV in my room. Nothing less than amazed, I took a seat on the edge of the bed to let it all sink in. Across from my room was a real bathroom with hot water and warm blankets. I could not recall the last hot shower I had taken. It was so hard to believe that a few days ago I was on a secluded island off Colombia, and now I was surrounded by such wealth. Knowing full and well that most Ecuadorians did not live under such extreme circumstances, I only wondered what the economic differences were in such a country.

Days 37-42: June 30-July 5, 2008

Quito, Ecuador

The next morning I awoke to a maid. She was there making me breakfast and coffee and had washed and folded all of my laundry. Quite possibly my mouth fell onto the floor when I entered the kitchen and saw her. A huge believer in Karma, I believed that was Karma's way of paying me back for all the stranded tourists I stopped to help in San Diego's Gaslamp District or led up to Balboa Park or told about free chocolate at Ghirardelli's. Whatever the circumstances, I was apparently living with one of the richest families in Ecuador. The maid even made my bed.

Leaving the house I had to go through the two gates. My host mom, Lucia, handed me a ring of keys over breakfast offering a mesmerizing concoction of entries to and from places. As I fit the keys into the gates it took me ten minutes to unlock myself. What types of dangers were they expecting in this neighborhood? Leading down the street I soon came face to face with Quito's *trole* system. A red subway system above ground, the *trole* was the most experienced public transit I had seen since leaving America. It was WAY ahead of the times and in fact made San Diego's public transit system look non-existent. Coming from a city that had been fighting over a trolley map for years, I found it unbelievable that a South American town could find the financing and architecture years before the world's wealthiest nation. For only twenty-five cents I took the *trole* line to Baca Ortiz, which is where my new Spanish school and Volunteer Ecuador office was located. Greeting people I had only met by email, I was excited to begin adding to my newfound language. Handing me a ten-page stack of Spanish gibberish, the professors attempted to give me a test to see what level of Spanish I was on. Unfortunately, it was mostly verbs in the past tense, which is exactly where I had left off in Nicaragua so I looked up and said, "I guess we will start here." The Equinox Spanish School in Quito was extremely different from Nicaragua. For starters, it stood behind a locked gate and came with real glass windows and a front door. Everything there was way too nice for me, traveling as a backpacker. The professors all dressed in business attire accessorized with the latest fashion scarves and boots. I had only backpacker clothes, such as jeans and hiking boots. I felt very out of place each day I entered.

Throughout the week I would find school less and less exciting. Each move I made brought criticism from the professors whether it was in my pronunciation techniques or misstep in letting an English word slip through. Losing the fun in learning the language, I found myself refusing to work on homework after hours and never opening up my textbooks. Ecuador Spanish was so different; it was as though I went from learning English in Alabama to Connecticut. *Irregulares verbos en el pasado.* That was where I had difficulty with my Espanol. Everything was very proper in Quito, and it was as though I was practicing on pins and needles. I found the way my teachers talked to be a joke. Having traveled and spoke Spanish for a month, I knew that no one talked like them in the real world.

Each morning I would study for two hours privately with my professor whose name I never learned in the five days I was there. The second half of school was spent in group study where we talked about typical Ecuador celebrations such as *Carnival* and *El dia de difuntos.* My teacher asked us to explain these days in our country. I thoroughly enjoyed the San Diego version of Mardi Gras. The words did not translate, and my professor did not understand why we do not have a Day of the Dead in the States. When I figured out she meant Halloween, I was on to it immediately. Both she and my group partner enjoyed learning about how small children go trick or treating, and candles line the sidewalks. Next, I got to discuss Christmas. My favorite holiday of all time, it was exciting to learn to speak about this in another language! I learned all kinds of new important words and explained how my mom makes a *jamón que pinas, papas casserole, maize casserole, coco pie*, and more. Mouths watering, my teacher now wanted to come over to my house. During group class we had to discuss where we lived and how much *dinero* was *necesito* to live for one month. It became clear to me that I did not know how anyone could afford to live in San Diego after my little budget exercise, and my professor and partner could not believe it cost thirteen-dollars to go to the cinema or that you could not just buy a CD on the street corner. I explained that there is sun all the time in SD, *no lluvia*, but after listening to their budget, I, too, believed we were nuts.

After class the first day, another professor presented me with a map and circled where my house was. Clearly I had no idea how to return since I was led to the *trole* that morning and dropped off by a taxi driver the night before. The professor explicitly told me at which trolley stop to get off; however, a recurring theme in Latin America, NO ONE THERE KNEW HOW TO GIVE DIRECTIONS. Therefore, she told me the wrong *trole* stop, and when I exited, there were no familiar sights. With nothing but a tree circled behind a park on a tourist map, I began walking up one of the many hills in Quito. I worked up a sweat and stripped off my down jacket, then soon rid myself of my second layer t-shirt. I ended up walking the hills of Quito for an hour. I was so lost and did not even know the address of my house. Crossing the street I recognized a street sign marked on the map, and suddenly thought I knew where I was. Attempting to take a shortcut, a dachshund jumped out and attacked me. Snapping his little jaws upon my ankles, he retreated moments before getting pepper sprayed. Nearing a community college, I noticed that

I was close to the circled tree on the map and cut around behind a building where I was met by nothing but a twenty-foot high wall and a great big black dog with snot dripping down his nose. Why did everyone in Latin America have a fucking dog anyway? I slowly turned around and retreated before becoming dog bait and after using all the water in my Camelback I huffed and puffed into the house. Seriously? That was not supposed to be a hike; I was just trying to get home from school.

Soon I figured out that I was living in the most affluent area around. All the people in my neighborhood drove expensive cars and did not work. After visiting the mall one afternoon, I discovered the stores were full of American name brands, such as GNC and Sunglass Hut. Also, one evening my host family had coffee and biscuits. I did not know anyone in the States that had coffee and biscuits and had yet to meet anyone in Latin America that did that either. My family did it while listening to opera music. It was a little awkward to have coffee and biscuits in my Appalachian State t-shirt. Even for me, who can adapt to anything.

Throughout the week I went to sightsee various parts of Quito including Old Town. Definitely a sight to see, it was full of plazas, parks, monasteries, and *iglesias*. I toured the Monastery of San Francisco, the city's largest colonial structure and its oldest church. Plaza Santo Domingo was like Horton Plaza or Times Square full of street performers, magicians, and little boys who would shine shoes. On the corner was the Church of Santo Domingo. Nearby was the Palacio del *Govierno*, or Presidential Palace, and it was surrounded by crowds eating ice cream, reading newspapers and soaking up the warm afternoon sun. I noticed a great little pastry shop so I popped inside and enjoyed a big slice of chocolate

cake for a measly eighty cents! Then two tourists asked me
for directions in Spanish. I guess I looked as if I knew what
I was doing, but really I was just as lost as everyone else; I
guess I just faked it better.

Later in the day I tried to go to the United States Embassy.
Walking down the street, that area of Quito was transformed
from sagging windowsills and dodgy ally ways to a sunshine
filled plaza surrounded by a Kentucky Fried Chicken and
McDonald's. The embassy was located directly behind the
McDonald's as if Americans in search of a replacement passport would be urged to pull over and fill up on Big Mac's.
Around the block I could not even get near the door because
of all the Ecuadorians waiting in line to obtain a United States
Visa. I simply wanted to follow-up about voting in November and found it interesting that American citizens could not
be let in without having to wait behind the long line of chaos.
I walked to the front where an Ecuador policeman pointed to
a website for United States Citizens who would be abroad in
November. That kind of took the fun out of my visit to an
American Embassy, but I thanked him just the same. After
logging on to the website, it did not work, defeating my pur-
pose of the visit and unnerving my faith in the United States
government. I was also wondering where the United States
military officials were that supposedly guard the doors of the
foreign Embassies.

Another afternoon I walked through the New Town and found
a place in Quito called *Gringo Land*. Then further on to
Mariscal Sucre where I popped into a restaurant and had a
full lunch for one-dollar and fifty cents. I continued wondering up Av Amazonas to Parque El Ejido, the equivalent to
Balboa or Central Park. Although there were some slides
there so high I would not dare try them. On the way back to

the trolley I stopped for some ice cream, then headed to the mall to study, since there were no *bibliotecas* close by and all the universities were private. At the trolley another guy asked me for directions, and I began to wonder if I had a sign on my back. While sitting at the café, I was approached by a man who asked me if I spoke English. He needed help with a school project and must interview an English speaker. After asking me about forty questions, including do I know anyone who plays a guitar and do I like Ecuadorian men, he helped me finish my *tarea,* and I wished him *Buenas Suerta* with his project.

I celebrated America's Independence Day south of the Equator. Even though I was not in the States, I decided to show my American pride by doing what every American should do when in a foreign country on the Fourth of July and went to patronize McDonald's. Dreaming about it for days, I was so tired of eating soup and rice. Sometimes one just has to have a hamburger. Entering the establishment it was packed to the brim, but not with Americans, and I whittled my way in to line. I attempted to order a Big Mac and a Coca-Cola, but the young man behind the register tells me they are out of both. Staring at him blankly I gazed up at the neon sign's flashing mouth-watering pictures of hamburgers and chicken nuggets. How could it be that a McDonald's was out of Big Mac's and Coca-Cola's? Two things the franchise was built on. Depressed, and a little upset to be an American, I settled for a Quarter Pounder and Coke Zero, definitely not the same impact. Passing my tray off, the McDonald's workers attempted to give me packs of mayonnaise instead of ketchup. When I asked for ketchup, they gave me one little pack; I told them I needed a lot more. This place was also so packed that finding a table was harder than finding a keeper in the online dating pool, and I was forced to settle for a seat in the very back. Tasting my Quarter Pounder, I wished I had turned around when they told me there were no more Big Mac's and sucking up the Coke Zero, I knew it would definitely be my last diet drink ever.

After McDonald's I headed to the Basilica del Voto Nacional, which was high on a hill in the Northeastern section of old Quito. Basilica del Voto Nacional was a church with two gothic towers. The adventurous one could climb to the top and cross a rickety wooden plank inside the main roof before climbing more steep stairs and ladders to the top. The Basilica stands 150 meters long, 35 meters wide, and 35 meters high in the Central Ship and 15 meters high in the votive chapels. Its towers are 78.23 meters high, 73 meters in the dome, 16 meters by 45 meters on the base of the towers. It has seven access doors. Acquiring a ticket for two-dollars, I entered the first tower and began up the sterile, concrete stairs.

Around each corner I encountered secret passageways, open for anyone to accidentally lock themselves in while looking for lost ghosts or fine artwork stashed inside the walls. Thick bars covered the windows, and when I arrived on the church's main floor I gained a spectacular view of the sun shining through the window pains, lighting up the altar and numerous crosses. A few flights up there were the ancient wooden planks. Secured only by two thin ropes on each side, I started across as my weight rocked the bridge from right to left. The hair rose on my arms as one misstep and I would be toast across these planks. At the end of the bridge I was met by a steep ladder, so narrow my backpack swiped both sides as I climbed up. It was very scary, but climbing up the clock tower was even worse. With each strenuous step I shook and prayed that I did not lose my footing and tumble over into old town Quito. Once I was at the top I breathed in quickly and asked another tourist to take my photo before hustling it back down. High up above town, the fear had set in, and I saw what I came for so now it was time to leave. Backing down, it was not easy to assess where my feet should land, and I traveled as slow as a snail. My plan was to not leave Quito on crutches.

I had heard about a Fourth of July party for Americans back towards *Gringoland* so I began to wander towards the main part of Quito. On the way I stopped at a *peliqueria* because I was in desperate need of a haircut. Now, there are a lot of reasons why it is important to know Spanish while traveling in Central and South America. The first is that at some point one will need a haircut and it is VERY important to tell them EXACTLY how one wants it cut. For $3/US I could get it cut and washed in Quito; for another $3/US, I could add a blow dry and style. So I decided to splurge and go all out. Before I knew it, Ugly Betty's sister had thrown me back in her salon chair and was washing my hair. There were pictures of Shakira everywhere, and J Lo was blaring through the speakers. I was staring straight ahead and praying I did not end up looking like either one by the time I left. Next, there was a straight razor in my hair, and the ends were being hacked off. I came out looking good, but I was panic-stricken for a while.

Further down the street, I attended the American Fourth of July party. Walking up, there was a cooler full of Budweiser and a grill stacked with hot dogs and hamburgers to help us feel as though we were back in the States. The only difference was the kids as young as eight approaching the table to sell us Chiclets and cigarettes. Staring into their tiny faces, I pondered who let these children have access to cigarettes? The guys gave them money which only caused more kids to show up. The crowd was made up of many United States travelers, a lot from Southern California. Over cold beers and warm burgers, we bonded with stories of local bars back home and favorite beach pastimes. It was nice to have that little bit of home, if only for one night.

Day 44: July 5, 2008

Otavalo, Ecuador

Saturday morning I woke up early for the journey to Otavalo, Ecuador. Known for their great marketplace, travelers and locals alike came from all over to experience Otavalo's famous giant Saturday market where traditionally dressed indigenous people sell their handicrafts. Getting there would require taking a two hour bus ride to see the goods within the city. After celebrating America's independence the evening before, 7:00 AM came early that weekend morning as I started packing my *mochila* before heading to the trolley and squeezing on. Barely able to fit through the sliding doors, I knocked several people out of the way corralling my way through and parking myself in a corner of the metro train, so as not to get my bag slashed or mugged on my way. I needed to go to the San Blas area of Quito, but my trolley line did not stop there, instead leaving me to back track some ten blocks. When I asked the policeman exactly where the area was, he wickedly smiled and asked me if I need a 'companion' to get me there. Laughing nervously, I thanked him and replied "no" as I continued on my way. Once I arrived at the San Blas Park, I dropped off my bags before hopping back on the trolley to the main Quito bus terminal. The bus terminal was huge, filled with numerous windows and street vendors, but we arrived right as the Otavalo bus was leaving. I had been waiting to visit Ecuador to buy some fun souvenirs so my excitement for the day was magical.

On the bus I quickly fell asleep and woke up to the Andean mountains overlooking a breathtaking lake. Spectacular views from high up in the mountain ranges offered postcard pictures as the bus teetered along the bumpy trail. When we pulled into Otavalo, I walked the streets until I stumbled upon numerous stands of chicken, *arroz,* and potatoes. Picking the one with the shortest line, we took a seat on a short wooden bench where the short, heavy-set Ecuadorian woman served up hearty bowls of potato soup. The plates and silverware were washed in nothing more than a bucket of brown water and I begged the question if there were even soap in the mixture. Accompanying the main plate was the traditional juice of sorts and on that day it was light yellow lemonade, which I drank down fast; however, Chris and Theresa opted to stick with bottled water. Finishing our lunch, we parted ways for a few hours to shop. Browsing down row after row of handmade crafts, my mind became exhausted from haggling over one or two-dollars and the dreams I had of leaving with an entire Christmas tree of gifts vanished. Finally, I settled on an alpaca sweater which I would wear in Cotopaxi and a beautiful new *bufanda*.

Late in the day I arrived back in Quito where I had no room plans yet for the night. I phoned over to Casa Bambu, a quaint hostel high up on a hill, which offered a great rooftop terrace to view the city. Sitting in the back of the taxi, I feared we may not make it up the hill, it was so steep, and wondered how I would walk up the road the next morning. After checking in at the front desk, it appeared I would have the whole hostel room to myself since it was slow season in Quito. Dropping my bags directly on the hardwood floor, I grabbed a few bananas from the little *tienda* down the street and made a quick supper of oatmeal before crashing after the long day.

Day 43: July 6, 2008

Quito, Ecuador

The next morning I woke up early and walked up the massive hill Casa Bambu was perched on, towards Parque Itchimbia. Parque Itchimbia contained 360-degree views of the city and was the perfect place to spend a nice, quiet Sunday morning. It had cycling and walking paths, as well as a dog park, numerous soccer fields, and an observatory for night viewings. I took several hours just to walk through the park and have some time to myself. After traveling for so long, it was nice to find a quiet park bench to enjoy some time alone and to take a breath and relax. Looking out at the city I simply reflected on my travels and my life. I was having a great adventure and experiencing many wonderful things. Yet, I had no one to share them with. All along the way I met friends and couples traveling the world together and I was the solo gypsy going down the road alone. Yesterday I received an email from a friend asking me if I had come to any realizations on my trip yet. I didn't know I was looking for any. What did she mean by that? Did all of my friends think I was lost in my life and out here trying to find myself? Why does someone always have to be lost...why couldn't I just be looking to have a good time away from my everyday grind? Was there something so wrong with living in the moment?

As I walked back down the hill, I walked through Parque La Alameda and into the Mariscal Sucre area of Quito. Both areas were completely desolate on Sundays. In another area, known as the Parque El Ejido, there were hundreds of street vendors who had set up stalls selling handicrafts and an art show lining the street. Hundreds of hand painted canvases decorated the sidewalks, and artists urged me to stop and look at their work. But I was on a different mission that day, to find some new tennis shoes to begin running again. I had not been able to run in Central America due to the heat, but I was looking forward to exercising in Ecuador as the weather was impressionably cooler. Since it was Sunday, though, most stores were closed, and after searching among several streets I was still empty of new *zapatos*. While I had come across a few open stores, I had not been able to track down my size. After explaining that I needed a USA size eight, they kept trying to give me a six. Desperate to sell me anything they could, I left frustrated and finally went home and took a nap. After waking up I headed back into the Old Town section where I tried on several pairs and finally bought a knock-off pair of Nike's for ten-dollars even though they were still a little too large. They would have to do for the next few months. It was necessary to help with all the ice cream I had enjoyed in Central America.

Day 44: July 7, 2008

Quito, Ecuador to Latacunga, Ecuador

I was scared. Sitting on the bed of a residential hotel in Latacunga, Ecuador, I found myself knowing that the only other people staying in the hotel would probably have to register on Meghan's Law in the USA. The guy in the room next to me had a prostitute with him, and I listened as he beat her before the sex began. I moved the table in front of my locked door and curled up under my sleeping bag which I had placed on top of the covers because there was no way in hell I would be touching the bed. Leftover pubic hairs donned the sheets and the smell of stale urine was so rank I almost moved to another hostel. I lay there in all my clothes, holding my pepper spray, afraid it was going to accidentally go off inside my bag and get me instead. I had no doubt the hotel was great for the local Ecuador guy, but for a single, blonde, American girl lying there that night I was scared as hell. Not to mention I had not seen one other tourist since I left Quito.

I wondered how in the hell I had exactly arrived in that position.

I had wanted to give back to the world. I had chosen to perform volunteer work on my journey. After traveling through Central America the first time around I knew I wanted to bring something more meaningful back from the second trip. I had chosen Ecuador to perform volunteer work because I had read great things about the volunteer organization. Volunteering with most organizations in South America involved some sort of stipend, and the Volunteer Ecuador program fit best into my budget. Offering whatever skills I had, I asked to be placed where I was needed the most. Prior to my arrival I had communicated via e-mail with the Volunteer Ecuador organization on numerous accounts. I had sent my resume to the director and filled out stacks of background information. A month before my trip, I was contacted via e-mail and told by Volunteer Ecuador they had found a program to place me in, located in the Cotopaxi region. Volunteer Ecuador did not offer much more information, other than I would be teaching some English, agriculture and athletics to women and children. The thoughts excited me. For years I had been a middle-man in politics, and now I was being offered an opportunity to work hands on. I was told there would be two other English-speaking volunteers, and we would each live with a local family during our time in the village.

The second day I was in Quito the project director visited the Equinox Spanish School to discuss the project guidelines with me. Speaking no English, he introduced himself to me and broke into a conversation completely in rapid Spanish. He then handed me all the project information which was entirely in Spanish. From the emails I had communicated prior to my arrival, I had assumed the project director would speak English. At least a little English. How did the volunteer program expect the leader to communicate with the English-speaking volunteers? My Spanish was okay by that point but not at a lifetime fluency level. Making out the translation with my professor, I came to understand that I would not live with a local family; instead, I would spend time in my own house in the village. While the village was technically in the Cotopaxi region, it was nowhere near the actual town of Cotopaxi, and the village was indeed four hours from the nearest town providing phone or Internet access. The school was also nowhere near ready to begin teaching classes.

Now that I sat on the dirty bed, I thought of all my friends who said "You can give back in the States." But, I had refused to listen to them saying there were other places in far greater need.

Earlier in the evening I ventured out in Latacunga after my *accompania*, first dropped me off. This had given me an hour to stay locked inside or venture around town. After thirty minutes I decided to look around Latacunga but quickly came back. Sighting no other white faces, I received mysterious stares. The streets of Latacunga were pitch dark and deserted. I scurried back to the front door of the hotel, where the entry was locked and a fierce dog could be heard behind it. Cracking the doors open and pulling him away, a shriveled elderly woman answered and asked who I was. I told her I was the girl in Room Fourteen and she let me up. I could not see anything. The hotel was completely dark and if someone was going to kill me, let them, because I could not see it coming anyway! And that was how I arrived curled up in my sleeping bag, lying scared, praying for tomorrow and daylight.

Day 45: July 8, 2008

Latacunga, Ecuador to Guayama Village, Ecuador

Last night's sleep was a nightmare. I kept waking up thinking I was:

1. Going to Die
2. Roll over on top of my pepper spray

There was no need for my TIMEX alarm as I was wide awake and packed by the time the project director, Miguel, came at 7:30 AM for breakfast. The shower was filled with cobwebs and spiders accompanied by leftover toilet paper and cigarette butts from the previous occupant so I did not even think about visiting the bathroom. Miguel walked me to meet his wife, Marisol, who was also associated with the project and their two-year-old daughter. She spoke no English either. She spoke Kichwa, an ancient Inca language still used throughout Ecuador, Peru, and other areas of the world. Breaking into each other's languages over breakfast, we began to dissect our lives. Sitting there I watched as a warm, gooey concoction was placed before me in a large glass. Until that day I believed I could eat anything, but that changed when I was given that hot drink in a glass. Using my spoon, I fished out the dark yellow color and sipped on it, tasting it slowly. It turned out to be the hard boiled part of an egg and some other mush to drink. There was no way; I could already feel my stomach regurgitating. I loved eggs, but that was not going to happen. I had recently heard a story of a girl who gained salmonella in Peru while hiking the Inca Trail after she ate an egg, and I was not taking any chances.

After breakfast I accompanied Marisol to the Ecuador Public Assistance office. The walls were filled with posters and photos of community service workers giving back to Ecuador. While sitting there taking it all in, another lady in line asked me to assist her with filling out her public assistance papers. I did not know if it was because I was white or what, but I just assumed she trusted me. By the time we left there, I was convinced Ecuador's public assistance program was infinitely better than America's. After we left, we met up with Marisol's brother-in-law and headed into the marketplace to buy some plastic chairs for the school we were to build. While children in America are worried about whether they're going to be in the overflow trailer, kids in Ecuador do not even have chairs on which to sit. Then we headed to purchase items for my room, such as a pillow and alpaca blanket before heading to the bus at 11:00 AM. The bus would not leave until 1:00 PM, but it was already getting busy, and we needed four seats. Grabbing some seats up front, I spent the extra two hours catching up on reading. Soon the bus filled with locals heading home to Latacunga for the night. Aisles were covered with rice and potato sacks; children were placed in any spare seat, and my backpack was used as a resting spot for a young boy who had been working in the marketplace all day. Shortly after noon, we left our sacks on the bus and walked across the bus gates to quickly take lunch near the station before we headed out. Leaving the station, the bus was the most packed I had seen since Guatemala. Women had their shirts pulled up to their necks and were breast feeding their children, guys were hanging to the roof top, and people were sitting on top of each other. No one smiled. They were all tired from work and travels. Leaving the outer limits of

Latacunga, the Andeans came into view; broad mountains, lined with tiny houses dotted far up in the hills. Every now and then the land flattened out, but for the most part the hills were reminiscent of an old 1970's carpet. A weird shade of green, with little patches of funky yellow thrown in.

The bus ride was scary. We turned corners with less then twelve inches between us and the edge of the mountain. I was scared a lot. I tried to focus on reading my book. There was no way. The ride was lengthy; over four-and-a-half hours and I was the only white person on the bus. People thought I was on the bus for the Quilotoa loop and kept trying to push me off, often times picking up my bag and passing it through the door. I explained that I was there to teach English and help set up a school. Explanations fell on deaf ears since many people did not even speak Spanish; they spoke Kichwa, a language I did not even know.

Leading up the mountains, the air was very cool, and I could not see where we are going. We were far up into the clouds. Leaning back in my seat to calm my fears, I heard something fly off the top of the roof. That could have been the bus. Instead, it was the metal makings for a door. Laughter erupted from the driver and ticket taker, but not from me. I saw the parts positioned far below us, down in a ditch. I did not move. What would happen if just one person moved, and the bus flew off the cliff?

Continuing higher up into the mountains, finally we arrived. We had been taken to a place where the road ended, and the journey continued only by foot. Cold weather hit me like a water hose. It was beyond frigid there. Dressed in a down jacket and beanie, my body shook all over, and I knew I had to unpack my long underwear fast. Stepping off the bus, people swarmed us. They all wanted to shake my hand and touch me. It was as though I was the President of the United States in a receiving line. My *acompania* from Quito to this small village was named Pedro, and he whispered for me to follow him, and we carried our market supplies into a damp, remote room, nothing more than a 10 x 10 box, which would be the school house. More people touched me all over. Then a young boy grabbed my backpack and led me on a path past fields of potatoes and maze.

I had no clue where I was going. He asked if I knew English. I told him, "yes, and very well." He said he wanted to learn, and I said that would not be a problem. After a fifteen minute walk through the rain and past a corn field, I was led to my house. Cement and bricks, it was basic. It was surrounded by three other buildings. It was a shock. I was in shock. I knew it was going to be basic, but that was beyond what I thought. Standing behind me was the whole village. Forty people crowded inside the house. They carried in vegetables, rice, and a small bag of apples. One man showed me how to use my camping stove and gave me my blanket. They wanted to know if I was okay. I said "yes."

It was a lie. I really had been sent to the middle of nowhere.

They left and I sat down on my bed. I breathed in heavily before beginning to make my dinner by my flashlight. That was what it was all about, right? Giving back to the less fortunate-I had a home to go back to in the US (okay, so maybe I gave it up to travel, but I had my mom's home to go back to!!). But, this was all they had.

I forced myself to believe my own words.

It is going to be a long three months.

Day 46: July 9, 2008

Guayama, Ecuador

Last night I lie there crying myself to sleep as the cold ripped right through my North Face sleeping bag as a hungry lion rips through raw meat. Layering my sleeping bag with the alpaca blanket, I covered every inch of my body and slept in a beanie and gloves. Light disappeared behind the mountains in Guayama around 7:00 PM, and on my first night I retreated to my home. Positioned there in the pitch dark, with the closest Internet and TV two hours away by foot, four hours away by bus, tears rolled down my cheeks. Not too often do I get lonely or emotional, but knowing that was my life for the next three months suddenly impacted me, and I snapped. I was not sure of the true distance, but the people I loved on the East and West Coast truly felt like a million miles away. Waking up the next morning, alone, in the same frigid cold, did not do much to calm my fears, but looking out at the Andean view was priceless. Deep valleys and high peaks were dressed in verdant greens and topped off with abundant wildflowers. All the villagers worked in the fields tackling projects such as burying potatoes or herding sheep.

My first morning I was invited to join a group of fellow volunteers, Spanish speaking teachers in for the day from Latacunga. Since the native tongue of the village was Kichwa, it was imperative for many villagers to learn Spanish in order to function in the marketplace and beyond. As I watched them bring Spanish into the lives of people, I was in awe at what little resources were provided within the school. No paper, pencils, or books. After class we went outside where the volunteers gathered everyone in a circle for a lesson on cultivating crops and environmentally friendly recycling. Taking products such as horse manure and chopped up purple wild-flowers, mixed in with molasses and urine, the volunteers taught local villagers ways to be resourceful.

On my first day in the village, I had guinea pig for dinner and horse for lunch. And for those of you reading this, about to throw up, do not say you would not have eaten it because guinea pig is an important food source in the Andean culture so I had to eat it. But God knows I wanted to throw up as it did not taste like chicken. Refusing the delicacy would have been a slap in the face to the family even though as I chewed on the meat it felt as though I was eating a melted Tonka truck fresh out of the microwave. The lunch excitement came when I accompanied the visiting Ecuador professors to a nearby village. The leader pushed me into the truck even though I had NO CLUE where I was going. I did not know if I was going back to Latacunga or to neighboring Chugchilan for Internet access. Twenty minutes down the road we spotted two girls walking through the rugged rocks and offered a ride. Turning backwards and continuing on five more minutes, we stopped in San Pedro, located in the Province of Cotopaxi. The Governor of Cotopaxi was in for the day and invited us to all have lunch together. It was just like having an old polit-ical lunch in San Diego except that I was wearing hiking boots, speaking Spanish and eating in an old pre-school. Food was available by the mounds, and there was way too much to handle. Attendees were slipping food into plastic shopping bags to take home. One at a time people could be spotted spooning potatoes and beef into their bags, positioned in their laps. I did the same, as 'When in Rome.' Following lunch the two girls we picked up had a line of people signed up for their project which was teaching people Spanish and how to deal with numbers in the marketplace. I was still amazed that I had been sent to a place where no one even spoke Spanish. Before coming to Ecuador the volunteer program emphasized my knowledge of Spanish, yet it seemed that Kichwa would have been a better fit. Standing in the crowd of people, I took the opportunity to start teaching English to a group of people. Some did not want to learn. They called it the *turismo* language. This upset me since I had been sent here for teaching purposes, but one can not force change nor force people to want to learn. Rain began to drizzle on our heads and we all piled back in the truck. A new friend had joined us for the ride and there were now seven of us in a little Dodge Dakota.

Once I arrived back in my village, I was greeted by the co-project director, Marisol. She instructed me to follow her. Again, I had no idea where I was going. On foot behind her, we hiked up a massive hill; everything in Guayama was of substantial consequence because each house topped out on a considerable Andean ridge. Once arriving at her home, it was nothing bigger than two twin beds that were shared by four children and her husband, Miguel. Marisol was still breast feeding her two-year-old daughter, but she started chopping wood like a lumberjack and requested that I pick out the guinea pig of my choosing. Shocked, I stumbled into the outhouse where the animals were kept and could not help but think of all my vegetarian friends back home who would have simply passed out in that moment. While she cooked, I taught the kids English in the dirt, starting with the alphabet, trying to remember all the symbols in my mom's kindergarten classroom. After choking down the soup, Marisol whispered something to me which I believed to be "stay here for the night," but her Kichwa and Spanish were so spliced with each other I did not understand a word coming out of her mouth. Moving my head from side to side, I told her I was okay and headed back down the giant mountain before the sun faded out. Thirty minutes later she banged on my door explaining something about cooking so I followed her again. It turned out she had some potatoes buried in a shack that she wanted to give me so now I felt like the bitch for not understanding the Kichwa language.

Day 47: July 10, 2008

Guayama, Ecuador

My day began at 8:00 AM by assisting Marisol in herding sheep from my village home up the mountain to her home. We first placed covers over the sheep's mouths and unpinned them from their caged fence in the lonely potato field, then led them towards the mountain trail. The vast Andean mountains affected me every day. I had to stop, take a breath, and a sip of water from my Camelback on the way up. Marisol and Miguel lived at the apex of a mountain overlooking Guayama Village, so the walk was steep. On the way she carried her wash load on her back and strolled along with ease while I struggled to maintain my posture. When we reached the house, I sat down again and was forced to catch my breath. Four children rushed over to me and shouted the alphabet letters I had taught them the night before in the dirt and with scraps of paper from my journal. They were overjoyed as they had been practicing all night and early morning.

Visiting with the children and taking in the view, I was joined by the other town villagers. A meeting was held and conducted over the money Pedro would need to travel to and from Quito the following day to pick up two more volunteers who would be coming to join the project. Everything in Guayama was a community event which I liked to think of as a city council meeting, sans the election process.

Following the meeting, Pedro asked if I would like to visit Chugchilan. There was a hostel there that he believed had Internet access. The village people stared strangely at me, for they did not know what the Internet was. Many of them were unfamiliar with computers. Longing for familiarity I enthusiastically replied, *"Vamos!"* I was not sure if we were hiking there, which I had been told was two hours by foot, or hitching a ride, because I did not spot any automobiles within radius. I grabbed my pack and began to follow Pedro. Walking it was, and we set out on foot. The group included me, Pedro, his eight-year-old nephew, plus a young friend, a ten-year-old girl named Ana and an elderly woman. They were all immediately kicking my butt on what one can only describe as a hike from hell. This path thing was often used by the indigenous people to go to and from Guayama to Chugchilan for different events, not for this Internet excursion. Pedro kept telling me the path was used by *turismos*, but I had been there for four days and had not seen a *turismo* yet. Every step brought a new challenge because the path consisted of nothing but me and an Andean ridge. Dangling near the edge, if I fell off no one would know for a long time as it would take the locals days to find the Embassy in Quito. Along our route we passed pigs, sheep, cows, petite houses where villagers worked the fields, and I struggled the entire way. I caused the group to rest more than once, but the thin air and high altitude were too tough for my body. Two hours later I crawled into Chugchilan, and Pedro ordered us two *pans* each and a frozen *helado*, which was nothing more than frozen ice and Kool-aid mix.

Further down the street, I left to go to the Black Sheep Inn because I had been told they had an Internet connection. The hostel is an extra .3 K hike out of town, but since I had made it that far, I dredged on. When I slowly ventured up the hill,

I was greeted by the American owner who told me the facilities were for guests only. Was he kidding? My face was red and puffy from the wind blowing against it, my hair was frizzy with delight, the bones in my body begged me to stop all this high-altitude hiking, and he would not allow me to use his computer. There was no use in explaining I just hiked two hours. For he said he was familiar with the hike and maybe the other town hostel would let me use their computer for five-dollars an hour. After a few moments of conversation, he sent me on my way saying he was glad to see me in Guayama because people always forgot about the village. That was the first I had actually heard anyone name the town. The entire time I believed I was in the town of Chugchilan. Turning back down the hill, I knocked on the door of Cloud Forest Hostel where I spotted an ancient computer and a dial up connection. Surrounded by my tour guides, the connection only brought up my Gmail in the old format. While typing and responding, all eyes were over my shoulder. While out in the daylight there was no privacy within the village, and it was so difficult to respond to email when ten people surrounded you. I could not even go to the bathroom alone; there were people waiting to shake my hand when I came out. As the week progressed, frustration took over and I began to lock myself in my house at all hours for a simple moment to myself.

Upon completion of my Internet time, the owner of Cloud Forest invited me to share lunch with her and her family. Following lunch, the Cloud Forest owner eagerly invited me to come back. I did not want to hurt her feelings, but I knew that hike was really a once in a lifetime thing. On the way back through the mountains, I had to stop every twenty minutes to catch my breath. Starring at me with frustration, I explained to the boys that people from California have a hard time acclimating to the high elevation in Ecuador. Halfway through I turned back to see how far I had come over the mountains and was astounded. I had never climbed that high in my life and was pretty sure I should have ropes or some sort of equipment guarding me along. When we arrived back in Guayama, word had spread that the *Gringa* had arrived. That was my official name in the village by that point even though I shared my name, spoke my name, and wrote my name with each villager. They consistently jumped up and down, chanting *Gringa, Gringa, Gringa!* It was a disgusting feeling to hear an entire village throw that word in your face. It felt like racism to me and I did not enjoy the way it made me feel. Like an outsider, one who did not belong. Frustrated, I was visibly upset each time one of them used the word *Gringo or Gringa*. It set me on a path thinking why I assumed it would be okay for white people to use the word in each other's presence, yet get upset when others spoke of it to them. In the eight days I spent in the village, only four young boys took the time to learn my name.

Void of necessary supplies such as books, paper, or pencils, I spent the evening teaching the boys English in the dirt. The project director was not living in the village, and plans to begin the project were disorganized, with no beginning date set. Unaware of what was really going on, I used my skills to the best of my ability and continued teaching the alphabet and English introductions such as "My name is _____. Nice to meet you." The smaller children asked me about numbers; they wanted to learn so they could charge tourists for hikes around the area. I had never been a teacher so I was unaware of where to begin. I had assumed that the project director would have some knowledge of how to lead a school, lesson plans, etc. Instead I was a blind horse, leading a blind horse. Everything I knew I had learned from volunteering in my mom's kindergarten class and was simply putting into play high up in the Andean mountains. For dinner that evening I took all the ingredients the villagers had given me and threw them in a pot. Seeing as how I forgot to backpack my Ecuador Recipes cookbook into Guayama I was hoping it would turn out okay. It made soup. There was no way I could live off soup and potatoes for three months. But at least it was not guinea pig. It was at that moment I realized I was a vegetarian living off soup and potatoes.

Day 48: July 11, 2008

On my fifth day in Guayama, three little boys, ages fourteen, ten, and eight, hiked me up to Laguna Quilotoa bright and early that morning. They appeared at my door ready to go before I had even made it out from under my alpaca blanket. Following them up another mountain, we hiked to a view so priceless that I wondered if National Geographic has seen it. Alfonso, 14, wanted so badly to learn numbers in English so he could charge tourists to go to the lake. But he hiked way too fast. Void of breath, I whispered to him that tourists could not go that fast. Creeping and crawling along, I was way too slow for him. Pouncing along like a mountain lion, he was at the top of one mountain while I lingered at the bottom. The other boys struggled behind me and talked about their brother in Spanish. Believing the extra weight from my backpack was a problem, Alfonso made his eight-year-old brother carry my Camelback, and his brother looked as if he were going to pass out. Alfonso had to take over. It was not a Camelback issue. This hike was demanding. Just when I believed it could not get any more physical or strenuous, it did. Quitting crossed my mind; I would just Google Image the lake pictures. Preparing to break the news to the boys, we then opened up into a field of flowers that reminded me of Texas Bluebonnets, and I decided to press on. With each rest stop,

I taught the boys more numbers. They had a hard time with four's as the F's and R's were difficult with their tongue. We spent time working on pronunciation and repeated one through twenty. I longed for beans or noodles, something to help me count out amounts and teach them, instead of just my fingers and dirt. Sitting near the top of Laguna Quilotoa, the boys shouted, "*Gringos* below," and I asked, "*Donde Está?*" My vision did not spot anything but sheep off in the distance, but they swore they spotted people. Explaining to them that Gringo was not a nice word, I took a few moments to teach them to say *turismos* instead. I also told them they were not allowed to call me *Gringa;* please say Jenifer. In agreement, we pressed on to the top.

As we summited Laguna Quilotoa, it was snowing lightly, and heavy freezing rain whipped hard against my face. Donning my down jacket, beanie, gloves, and long underwear underneath it all, I snapped a few photos and took off. I spent so little time there, and the visibility was so poor I left not really even knowing how big the lake actually was, only that I had made it to the top.

Back at home, Jason arrived. All 6′5" of him. A skinny, eighteen-year-old, white boy, from Kansas, Jason looked as though he skipped basketball practice with the Kansas Jayhawks to come to Ecuador. Pedro hauled Jason off the bus with his wheeled luggage. The first wheeled luggage I had seen since leaving the LAX airport. Jason was wearing converse sneakers and a sweatshirt. He did not possess a jacket. He was there to assist me in teaching English supposedly for a year, but I could tell by the immediate shock on his face that was not going to happen. I guided him to our cement home where he did a double take.

After Pedro dropped his bags and left, Jason asked me some questions, i.e.:

Jason: Where is the shower?

Me: There is no shower; there is a creek and one spout of running water for our house to share with three others. This morning I filled up a bucket and took a sponge bath.

Jason: What do we eat?

Me: We eat rice, potatoes, and soup. Can you cook? We have a stove.

Jason: No, I don't know how to cook.

(In my head I was now thinking that the village and Volunteer Ecuador were under the impression that I was supposed to cook for Jason for the next three months).

Jason: Where do we wash our clothes?

Me: I have been wearing the same clothes for seven days. There is a creek where the ladies wash their clothes, and they hang them out to dry.

Some more words about Jason. He was eighteen and fresh off the farm. It was safe to say he was definitely 'not in Kansas' anymore. He flew straight from his mother's house to Quito where he went wild and partied for three days until 6:00 AM every morning so when I told him we awoke at 6:00 AM and herded sheep and hiked, he did not take to the idea. Immediately upon his arrival, Jason said he might go back to Quito, and he had only been in Guayama for one hour. Walking into the kitchen, he reached for my *Nalgene* bottle and attempted to take a swig from it. Shocked and dismayed, I told him that was my personal water bottle, and he might want to use his own for hygiene reasons. Confused, he replied "What do we drink from?" I asked him, "didn't you backpack a water bottle?" He told me no, besides his clothes all he brought was a flask and a guitar. No harm there, except the flask was empty. Who packs an empty flask? Especially when they were going to the middle of nowhere for three months? My mind was wondering if I could really live with the young man for three months when he asked me to show him the town. Explaining to him that there was no town, simply a village of forty-two houses sprawled over hundreds of acres I wondered if he had read any of the material provided to us by Volunteer Ecuador.

As the sun went down over the Andean mountains, creating a purple glow into the night, I made the two of us dinner, sort of like a hospitable thing on his first night. During dinner Jason told me he was in shock. I explained that it would go away. He said he did not know how I spent a week there by myself. Again, I think I don't know how I will able to spend three months with him. There are a lot of activists in the world with half-a-brain and a nice ass. Brad Pitt automatically came to mind, but I had also seen George Clooney and Leo DeCaprio throw on a shirt for a good cause. Volunteer Ecuador could have sent me them, but they sent me Jason. Thanks.

Day 49: July 12, 2008

Guayama, Ecuador

The wind was blowing so hard the next morning that it cut through the tin roof, and rain dripped onto my head, waking me up. I snuggled back under the covers for a few more minutes and then drug myself up. It was going to be cold. Slipping out of the covers, I hurried into my jeans and boots fast and headed off to wash last night's dishes, which were Jason's responsibility, yet had somehow gone undone. There was no water so I was forced to wash everything with the bucket of rain water. As I began to prepare my last stash of oatmeal that I had backpacked, Jason crawled out of bed and enthusiastically inquired about having oatmeal for breakfast. I told him the oatmeal was mine, but he had leftovers from the night before. I did this for two reasons:

1. I did not want him to think I would be cooking for him for three months.

2. He did not eat all his dinner the night before so there were leftovers he needed to finish because food in Guayama was so scarce and we did not have a fridge so it would go bad.

Being a weekend day, after breakfast I spent most of the day hiking and studying although it was not as easy as it sounds. Every time I set off to hike the villagers followed me asking *"A Donde Va,"* and offering to send an *accompania* with me, when all I really wanted was five minutes to myself to listen to my I-POD for some English speaking company. Anytime I sat down to study there were little boys staring at me to see what the American was going to do next. Finally, I ended up barricading myself in my room which was cold and dark, but at least there were not fifteen villagers following me down a road asking me *"A Donde Va?"* The answer to that question was nowhere; there was nowhere to go but higher up into the Andean mountains. If one did not make it on the 3:00 AM bus to Latacunga, one was stuck in Guayama village all day long. It was on that day that I had reached a point. Between the villagers following my every move, and Jason, I did not know how much longer I was going to make it there. Far away from civilization, living with people who made fun of me, when I was there to help them, with an eighteen-year-old who did not know right from left, I was exhausted. Life was not supposed to be easy, but I had decided to take one year off, and this was not how I wanted to be spending it. I was unhappy and depressed up on a secluded mountain in Ecuador.

There is a place so lonely that no one knows unless they, too, have been there. High up in the Andes where the sky turns from blue to purple to midnight black and the stars take over, there is loneliness. The calm quiet was my only friend and I counted my days on a homemade calendar which I drew up by looking at my watch and crossed off each morning. I imagined what my friends and family are doing back home, but never did I imagine that they were imagining me. Could they even know what kind of life I was living, that I was herding sheep up a mountain or shelling peas to make homemade soup, when peas at the local grocery costs forty-five cents? It was so hard to believe those things existed, even in a world where we use the word recession because Americans have become so accustomed to such an easy lifestyle that to imagine shelling peas for a potato soup dinner would be the worst for some people, yet for the lives of Incas high up in the Andes, it was just another day in the life.

Day 50: July 13, 2008

Guayama, Ecuador

The following day Pedro said we would go to Chugchilan by car. But it turned out to be another hike. There was no way I could hike there again so I wished them good luck and spent the day alone and I studied Spanish. After a few hours, my neck hurt from looking down so often. Spying the pantry items in the corner, I could not eat soup anymore so I opened a can of tuna that I had been saving for this occasion. Then I took a walk out of the village for some fresh air, but not before a group of followers was behind me shouting *"A Donde Va?"* At 3:00 PM I walked up to the schoolhouse because Miguel was in the village and had called a meeting to discuss our project. But he did not show up until 4:30 PM. Around 5:00 PM the meeting got started with introductions even though the eight people at the meeting were all cousins and had known each other since birth. When Miguel began discussing the project, he addressed only Jason. It was as though I was not even in the room. Miguel did that at dinner the night before as well. Never fond of not being addressed, or dis-respected, all of this really irked me when the boy was eighteen.

During the meeting when Miguel spoke, I responded and said, "Yes" exactly when Jason did; however, all the men laughed at me as though I do not understand what is going on. Four hours into the meeting I excused myself since Jason and I were bound for the 3:00 AM bus to Latacunga in the morning. The meeting had drug on for hours, and the project was not ready to go at all. Together, both Jason and I had both concluded that the village people told one story to Volunteer Ecuador so they could get some volunteers to Guayama, then Volunteer Ecuador told us another story. At any rate, there would be no supplies, no pencils, no paper, and no books for months. It would be continuing to teach in the sand, but no one knew when the real start date would be. Food would continue to be potatoes and soup three times a day, a nutrition and health issue. There would be no Internet in Guayama until years from now, which also worried me because of my medical needs.

Sometimes things don't turn out like you thought. I was a strong person, but even strong people break down. Being up on that mountain, alone, did something to a person. It was mentally and emotionally exhausting. Before I traveled to Ecuador I did a massive amount of research to make sure it was a project I could commit myself to. Now that I was there it is sad to say I could not commit, because who knew when the next person would be back. It was hard to turn my back on something. It made me feel like a quitter, but when the project outline is not what was described I began to think the best thing to do was leave and let someone else come back when all the objectives were in place.

Day 51: July 14, 2008

Guayama, Ecuador to Latacunga, Ecuador

Waking up long before the sun did, it was 3:00 a.m. that Monday morning in Guayama as I walked to the bus in the pitch dark. Guarding the bus stop were two rabid dogs heading to attack me. I shook my pepper spray at them and Jason said "No, don't hurt the dogs." Obviously, Jason had never been to Guatemala, and he liked to get bitten. That kid was never going to make it up there. The bus took four hours to get to Latacunga so we could use the Internet. Upon arrival, I scoured the town for an open Internet Café, but no business would open until two hours after the bus dropped me off. Right at opening time, I logged online and called my mom and cried into the computer, relaying to her the situation far up in the Andes. She said to come back to the States. I had pretty much already made up my mind, but I just needed someone else to say it. I knew that another two months on the mountain would be so mentally draining on me that I just could not do it.

I had no way of knowing what tomorrow would bring, but I knew what I had to do today.

Epilogue

I left Guayama the next morning on the 3:00 AM bus and returned to the States one week later. My months of traveling had brought me countless new friends, thousands of priceless photographs, and a journal full of unforgettable memories. Although some people would label me as a quitter for the way the trip ended, I considered myself brave for other things I had done such as crossing borders, riding chicken busses, and testing my physical endurance. Traveling as a single woman through the world is a dangerous journey. But, what would a person be without trying.